DECRYPTING THE SECOND AMENDMENT

Interpreting the 2nd Amendment and surrounding arguments

Harley Robertson

Copyright © 2023, 2024 Harley Robertson

All rights reserved. Except for brief excerpts used in reviews, no portion of this work may be reproduced without express permission from the author or the author's agent.

Introduction

This book owes its existence to two seemingly unrelated catalysts. One is over two years of intense online debates with people about the meaning of the Second Amendment, many of which claimed to be constitutional lawyers, doctorate-level legal students, current or previous members of various US Armed Forces, or members of various State Militias such as the National Guard. The other catalyst is that I started writing a book about a much larger scope – how to understand American politics and the US Government. The problem is that both things were going on simultaneously, so while trying to write an article on this subject based on those social media conversations… I accidentally wrote a book about the Second Amendment.

I have been studying the US Constitution, including the Second Amendment, off and on for over thirty years, so when I began these online arguments, it was from what I thought was a moderately informed perspective. I found that many people passionate about their Second Amendment rights had no idea what that meant. For example, in 2022, some Canadians (the Freedom Convoy) protested in Ottawa, saying their Second Amendment rights should not be infringed upon. In Canada, depending on how you view their constitutional history, the Second Amendment has something to do with allowing the province of Manitoba to join Canada (https://www.justice.gc.ca/eng/rp-pr/csj-sjc/constitution/lawreg-loireg/p1t21.html).
Individual Canadian rights are protected through their Charter of Rights and Freedoms. The Charter of Rights and Freedoms does not mention personal ownership of arms, or militias, and it is not separated into amendments.

While I have spent hundreds of hours reading The Federalist Papers, Congressional Legislation, Supreme Court Opinions, and other constitutionally related information, I do not have a formal legal degree. I am just an American who has always been interested in how my government works and how it came about. I say always, but it probably started in High School and was sparked by my teacher Judie Cagle Kohler, who we lovingly called Coca-Kohler. My first degree was in 'Computer Information Management.' I've spent decades developing databases, software systems, and detailed analytical reports and visualizations to accurately represent data so that data can drive decisions, such as improving patient outcomes in medical institutions. I take that analytical approach to understand the US Constitution and the law. I believe that the research comes before the conclusion. You can't start researching any topic with the intent to cherry-pick data (or quotes and references). I will say upfront; please forgive my inclusion of excessively long quotations from the Framers, the Supreme Court, and others – it was an attempt to provide the full context of the words that were spoken and to avoid the appearance of cherry-picking myself. I put direct quotes in *italics*. The best example of where this makes a difference is probably the George Mason "we are all the militia" quote which is often used to imply that he was saying everyone always is in the militia, but when you take in his longer speech you realize he was talking about how the militia shouldn't be class-based. I was actively seeking not support for any particular interpretation of the Second Amendment but any shred of evidence that proved or disproved any existing theories on the topic.

Despite a lot of nonsensical arguments like "The Second Amendment is a right," where I had to respond by trying to explain that an Amendment is a change or addition to an existing document and how The Second Amendment discusses a right it isn't a right itself (yes, I am annoyingly precise and nit-picky when it comes to understanding law) – I did gather a greater understanding of the various interpretations and the inconsistencies in what various people think the

Second Amendment means. I tried to include as many of those perspectives as I could.

I should disclose that as much as I believe that data comes before conclusions, and I took that approach in my research of this topic, my initial belief was always that the wording of the Second Amendment makes its intentions self-evident. Thus, there was a slight bias in my research and those conversations, where I looked harder in trying to disprove what I had always believed the Second Amendment to mean than I did in trying to disprove other views based on the same principles many apply to their scientific research where they try to disprove their initial hypothesis. Thus, most of my online arguments started with "I think my understanding is correct – prove me wrong." While I couldn't help the fact that I already had an understanding of what the Second Amendment meant before I started this project, my goal with this project was to be willing to disprove that stance by being open to every argument against it. Along the way, I learned a great deal from those disagreements and conversations about how the US Military, State Militias, and the Selective Service are structured from people with a wide variety of perspectives on the topic. My views and understanding of the Second Amendment most certainly changed and evolved through this process.

There also may be a lot of repetition of the same arguments or information, as I tried to encapsulate topics so that the reader isn't expected to have everything from earlier passages memorized. Again, I apologize; despite the length of this discussion, my goal wasn't to write a novel but to provide clarity on this topic.

Thanks to those who generously proposed corrections and also those who argued against everything I said. This book would not be complete without you.

I hope you find the following informative, no matter how you interpret the Second Amendment. I've provided an extensive list of references at the end so that you can verify everything here.

Harley Robertson

The Second Amendment

The Second Amendment to the US Constitution states:

A well regulated Militia, being necessary to the security of a free State, the right of the people to keep and bear Arms, shall not be infringed.

This one sentence has caused a great deal of debate over the two centuries since it was added. Two primary interpretations are The Individual Rights Theory and The Collective Rights Theory. These names were established primarily after the 1939 United States v. Miller Supreme Court case. Neither says that individual rights do not exist.

If we were to re-word the Second Amendment to be more clearly aligned with The Individual Rights Theory, it would look something like this:

Being necessary for personal Defense, the right of people to keep and bear firearms, shall not be abridged.

If we were to re-word the Second Amendment to be more clearly aligned with The Collective Rights Theory, it would look something like this:

A militia trained by the States according to the discipline prescribed by Congress, being necessary for a State to execute the law, repel invasions, and suppress insurrections; the right of the people to a well regulated State militia, shall not be infringed.

There is also The Insurrectionist Theory, which is that the Second Amendment allows US citizens to overthrow the government. This idea was phrased by Florida Congressman Matt Gaetz as the Second Amendment *"being about maintaining within the citizenry the ability to maintain an armed rebellion against the government."* This theory is debunked by the

US Constitution, which says that Congress can suppress insurrections. The Constitution provides a framework for resolving our differences in how the government should work peacefully, without violence. The Second Amendment does not change that.

The State Militias, or National Guard of <state in question> as most people know them. The National Guard claims 1636 as its birth year, when the militia was founded in Massachusetts, though there were militias established before that through the English militia system, such as the Virginia militia established in 1607. We did not start operating under the US Constitution until 1789, so by that point, the militias were well established. The Militia Acts of 1792 empowered the President to call upon the State Militias when needed at a Federal level. Congress could do that because Article 1 Section 8 says that Congress has the power *"To provide for calling forth the Militia to execute the Laws of the Union, suppress Insurrections and repel Invasions."* The Militia Act of 1903 renamed the *"regularly enlisted, organized, and uniformed active militia in several States and Territories and the District of Columbia"* to *"national guard."* It continues to describe how those militias shall be well-regulated, such as being arranged into divisions that the State legislatures direct, how the highest officer ranks are arranged, and that they must follow the system of discipline and field exercise of the regular US Army.

The Militia Acts also mention the *"unorganized militia,"* but they were not talking about state militias as unorganized. They were talking about those who would qualify as being pulled into the militia should there be a need to call forth the Reserve Militia. In other words, the unorganized militia mentioned in the Militia Acts includes those not currently part of the US Armed Forces or part of the well-regulated (organized) State Militias. The unorganized militia (able-bodied men 17–45 as per 10 U.S. Code § 246) discussed in the Militia Acts closely mirrors who is mentioned in the Selective Service Act (currently men

18–26, but it was 18–45 at one point). The Selective Service Act allows the Federal Government to raise an article through conscription. The authority for the government to do so is from Article 1, Section 8, which says that Congress has the power *"To raise and support Armies."* They do so through the Selective Service System and can be initiated by the President issuing a draft order. Those in the Constitutional militia cannot be drafted through Selective Service, as they are called forth as part of the militia when needed for Federal Service.

From the US Constitution, Article 1 Section 8: Powers of Congress:

To raise and support Armies, but no Appropriation of Money to that Use shall be for a longer Term than two Years;

To provide and maintain a Navy;

To make Rules for the Government and Regulation of the land and naval Forces;

To provide for calling forth the Militia to execute the Laws of the Union, suppress Insurrections and repel Invasions;

To provide for organizing, arming, and disciplining, the Militia, and for governing such Part of them as may be employed in the Service of the United States, reserving to the States respectively, the Appointment of the Officers, and the Authority of training the Militia according to the discipline prescribed by Congress;

Major General James Parker

US Army 1876-1918

Head of Militia Affairs 1903-1908

Lieutenant-Colonel James Parker, while writing a summary of the Militia Act of 1903, addressed the concern that the act would impact a State's right to a militia:

There seems to be an impression in some quarters that this Militia Act of 1903 weakens the power of the States over the militia, and is in some respects an attack on State sovereignty. Nothing could be further from the facts. The bill is carefully drawn to preserve the authority of the Governors over their own troops, by "reserving to the States respectively the appointment of the officers and the authority of training the militia according to the discipline prescribe by Congress." In time of peace, the National Guard of each State is thoroughly a State force, made more efficient for that purpose than ever before by the aid of the general Government.

State Militias also often exist beyond the National Guard, even though the National Guard may be the only one that receives regular federal funding as per Congress's power to provide for the militia. Other state defense forces are funded under the sole authority of a State government. The Federal Government is not constitutionally prevented from "providing for" those other state defense forces, so they could decide to pass a new law at any point to make funding available to them. Considering they already provide the National Guard with billions of dollars annually, it's unlikely.

Congress has decided, expressed in 32 U.S. Code § 109 (c), to use its power to "call forth the militia" only with the National Guard. Other state defense forces won't be called into service as a whole by the Federal Government. However, unlike active National Guard members – they would not be exempt from a federal draft. Additionally, 32 U.S. Code § 109 (e) bars members of any reserve component of federal armed forces (including National Guard members) from joining one of these state defense forces. Again, Congress is not limited by the US Constitution from changing the law to allow for calling forth state defense forces into federal service.

This book focuses on US history, how the Second Amendment has been interpreted over time, and how the Supreme Court has weighed in on it through the many cases people claim are about the Second Amendment (if they are, or aren't).

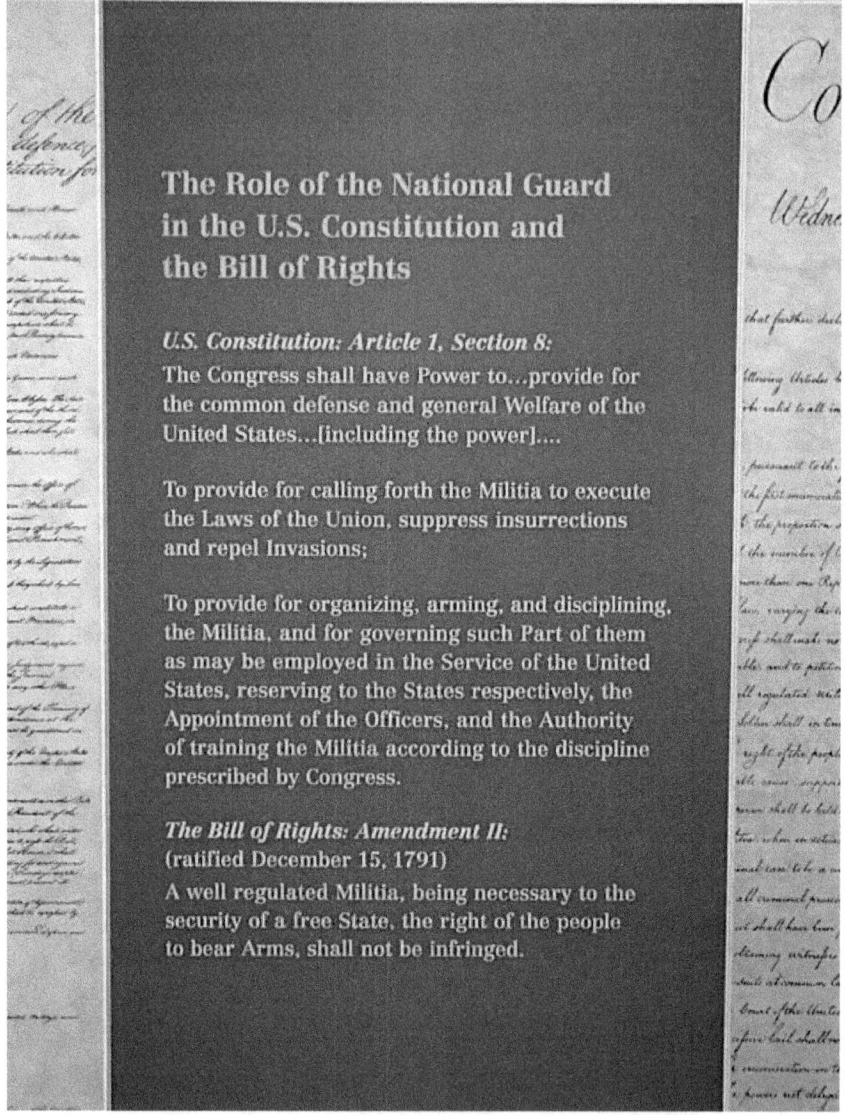

Photo from the National Guard Memorial Museum in Washington D.C.

In the Beginning

A journey from the first colonial militias to the American Revolution

The militias in the United States were not created by any portion of the US Constitution, in fact at the time of the American Revolution they were the result of two hundred years of military experience in the American Colonies, and a residual fear of standing armies born of European experiences. The Colonial Militias performed a variety of functions, were often formed of conscripted citizens (outside of Pennsylvania), and usually reported to the Colonial Legislatures (not the Governors). The quality and capability of these militias often fluctuated based on the need, when there were no immediate threats, they often fell apart from neglect. Many militias were small and reported to the local towns rather than the colony as a whole, especially in northern colonies. Southern colonies were a little more widely dispersed and had the additional function of maintaining slave populations.

Pocahontas

1596-1617

Daughter of Powhatan paramount chief, Wahunsenacawh

Also known as Matoaka (given name) and Lady Rebecca

In 1607 the English colonists of Virginia formed a militia of citizen soldiers to combat the Native Americans in the lands where they were establishing settlements. Until 1614 and the marriage between Pocahontas and one of the colonists, the colony was in a regular state of conflict with the local Powhatan warriors without a true standing army. The English Crown didn't control the colony until 1624 when they moved to establish a more organized standing militia system. Nearly all males between 16 and 60 were conscripted into this militia.

There are similar stories in other early North American colonies, the colonists created local militias to protect the settlements they were establishing, often at the instruction of whatever nation they reported to.

Diorama of the First Muster
displayed at the National Guard Memorial Museum in D.C.
by Andrew Chernak

On December 13, 1636, the Massachusetts court established the first militia regiments as we know them today in North America. Four of those regiments are still active today as part of the Massachusetts Army National Guard.

The colonial militias played a major role in the French and Indian War between 1754 and 1763. France was trying to block

English expansion, and General George Washington was sent from Virginia to demand the French to withdraw. In 1755 the Pennsylvania Assembly passed their first militia law, different in that their militia was voluntary and militiamen could return home every three days. By 1757 though, their militia system was more similar to those of the other colonies.

After the French and Indian War, there was a greater animosity between colonists and the colonial militias and Britain and the British regulars. Americans didn't like the oppressiveness of the British troops, or having to quarter them in their homes without consent. The American colonies had fared on their own primarily through the power of militias for more than 150 years, and they didn't appreciate the sudden presence of the British troops which remained after 1763, beyond their perceived necessity. In 1765, the British Parliament raised colonial taxes and increased requirements to house and supply the British Army. General Gage of the British Army said in 1772 that *"democracy is too prevalent in America."* Civil unrest only grew from there, with the "Boston Tea Party" in 1773, and a Continental Congress established in 1774.

One of the first actions of the Continental Congress was to resurrect the militias of the French and Indian War and convert them into a reliable army to oppose the British. They forced all officers to resign, to purge British loyalties, and formed the militias of thirteen colonies into the Continental Army, to be led by George Washington, as the Commander-in-Chief.

Thomas Gage

Military Governor of Quebec 1760-1763

Commander-in-Chief, North America 1763-1775

Governor of the Province of Massachusetts Bay 1774-1775

The final catalyst that started the American Revolution was a conflict between the militia of Massachusetts and General Gage. The General sent in troops to disarm the local militia six miles outside of Boston by seizing a local cache of gunpowder and weapons. By the time the Redcoats got there, the locals had already removed much of the gunpowder, but the action outraged the colonists who quickly started organizing the militias against the British Armies. General Gage was ordered to put down the rebellion by force, and so things continued to escalate leading to colonies individually declaring their independence from Great Britain.

Founding a Nation of Nations

George Mason

Virginia House of Burgesses 1758-1761

Virginia House of Delegates 1786-1788

George Mason wrote the Virginia Declaration of Rights, adopted on June 12, 1776. It states:

That a well-regulated militia, or composed of the body of the people, trained to arms, is the proper, natural, and safe defense of a free state; that standing armies, in time of peace, should be avoided as dangerous to liberty; and that in all case the military should be under strict subordination to, and governed by, the civil power.

The militia isn't all the people; it is of the people (you must be enrolled in the militia to be in the militia). They are trained to use weapons and are under strict subordination to and covered by the civil power (the people). The Framers (those who participated in the writing of the US Constitution, and Bill of Rights, as opposed to the Founders which is a broader term that applies to all that helped found the United States as an independent nation) also made a clear distinction between the militia and standing armies. The militia are part-time soldiers who are regular citizens the rest of the time – they report to the State, while standing armies are full-time soldiers – they report to the Federal Government. Many states had similar documents and similar wording.

Thomas Jefferson wrote the Declaration of Independence,

drawing upon the Virginia Declaration of Rights for the opening paragraphs. The Continental Congress ratified the Declaration of Independence on July 4th, 1776.

The Continental Congress adopted the United States Articles of Confederation in 1777 (the precursor to the US Constitution), which was ratified in all states by 1781.

This new independence from Great Britain allowed for alliances with France and foreign military and financial aid in the war. In 1783, Great Britain recognized the United States as a sovereign nation with the Treaty of Paris.

The new nation of the United States quickly realized the flaws in The Articles of Confederation, primarily that it did not give enough powers to the Federal Government which had no central leadership, no national court system, no power to tax or regulate trade, and an ineffective legislative system.

The Articles of Confederation created a loose association between the states but declared that each state retains its sovereignty and independence. Many of the themes currently in the US Constitution were there, such as the Freedom of speech and debate in Congress. Article 6 limited State powers, such as saying that no body of forces can be kept up in time of peace, unless allowed by the United States, but every State "*shall always keep up a well-regulated and disciplined militia, sufficiently armed*" and equipped. Article 7 said, "*When land forces are raised by any State, for the common defence, all officers of, or under the rank of colonel, shall be appointed by the legislature of each State respectfully.*" Nothing in the Articles of Confederation mentions personal gun ownership.

By 1786 there were calls for the Articles of Confederation to be replaced by something which gave the Federal Government more authority. The US Constitution was written in 1787 to address those concerns. It firmly established three branches of the Federal Government and outlined the powers and restrictions of each of them.

On September 17th, 1787, there was a convention with delegates from New Hampshire, Massachusetts, Connecticut, New York, New Jersey, Pennsylvania, Delaware, Maryland, Virginia, North Carolina, South Carolina, and Georgia present. The US Constitution was signed by 39 delegates.

Debating Amendments

When the US Constitution was introduced, there were two major political factions. The Federalists, who were fine with the Constitution as is and wanted it adopted without change, and the Anti-Federalists who felt it gave too much power to the Federal Government and wanted to add restrictions to federal power, such as the English Bill of Rights of 1688. A point made by the Federalists was that enumerating rights in the Constitution would leave the government open to infringing upon all unenumerated rights. They weren't completely sold on the effectiveness of the English Bill of Rights. Some made the argument that a Bill of Rights would result in the people having fewer protected rights, not more. Their perspective was that powers should be included in the Constitution, and all legislation after must have a basis from that rather than trying to list everything the government can't do.

Alexander Hamilton

New York Militia 1775-1776

Continental Army 1776-1782

Congress of the Confederation 1788-1783

US Secretary of the Treasury 1789-1795

United States Army 1798-1800

On January 10, 1788, a few months after the US Constitution was signed, the Daily Advertiser published "Concerning the Militia" by Alexander Hamilton (also known as Federalist 29), where he made the case as to why a State-controlled Militia is essential. He begins by framing a debate that was going on at the time over Article 1 Section 8 of the Constitution, which says that the Federal Congress can call up on the militia to repel invasions and suppress insurrections and "*To provide for organizing, arming, and disciplining, the Militia.*"

Hamilton writes:

It being therefore evident that the supposition of a want of power to require the aid of the POSSE COMITATUS is entirely destitute of color, it will follow, that the conclusion which has been drawn from it, in its application to the authority of the federal government over the militia, is as uncandid as it is illogical. What reason could there be to infer, that force was intended to be the sole instrument of authority, merely because there is a power to make use of it when necessary? What shall we think of the motives which could induce men of sense to reason in this manner? How shall we prevent a conflict between charity and judgment?

He was addressing complaints that Article 1 Section 8 was insufficient to clarify the need for and organization of the militias which speaks to the reason why an amendment on the topic may have been warranted.

Hamilton explains the importance of a militia being well-regulated and what that means, such as training at a state level instead of a national level, having them properly armed and equipped, and having them assembled once or twice a year.

The project of disciplining all the militia of the United States is as futile as it would be injurious, if it were capable of being carried into execution. A tolerable expertness in military movements is a business that requires time and practice. It is not a day, or even a week, that will suffice for the attainment of it. To oblige the great body of the yeomanry, and of the other classes of the citizens, to be under arms for the purpose of going through military exercises and evolutions, as often as might be necessary to acquire the degree of perfection which would entitle them to the character of a well-regulated militia, would be a real grievance to the people, and a serious public inconvenience and loss. It would form an annual deduction from the productive labor of the country, to an amount which, calculating upon the present numbers of the people, would not fall far short of the whole expense of the civil establishments of all the States. To attempt a thing which would abridge the mass of labor and industry to so considerable an extent, would be unwise: and the experiment, if made, could not succeed, because it would not long be endured. Little more can reasonably be aimed at, with respect to the people at large, than to have them properly armed and equipped; and in order to see that this be not neglected, it will be necessary to assemble them once or twice in the course of a year.

He makes the case that having a well-trained militia would be easier to maintain and require smaller military establishments.

By thus circumscribing the plan, it will be possible to have an excellent body of well-trained militia, ready to take the field whenever the defense of the State shall require it. This will not only lessen the call for military establishments, but if circumstances should at any time oblige the government to form an army of any magnitude that army can never be formidable to the liberties of the people while there is a large body of citizens, little, if at all, inferior to them in discipline and the use of arms, who stand ready to defend their own rights and those of their fellow-citizens. This appears to me the only substitute that can be devised for a standing army, and the best possible security against it, if it should exist.

Hamilton concludes with the reasoning as to why militias should be under the authority of the State and not the Federal Union:

In times of insurrection, or invasion, it would be natural and proper that the militia of a neighboring State should be marched into another, to resist a common enemy, or to guard the republic against the violence of faction or sedition. This was frequently the case, in respect to the first object, in the course of the late war; and this mutual succor is, indeed, a principal end of our political association. If the power of affording it be placed under the direction of the Union, there will be no danger of a supine and listless inattention to the dangers of a neighbor, till its near approach had superadded the incitements of self-preservation to the too feeble impulses of duty and sympathy.

James Madison

Colonel, Orange County, Virginia Militia 1775-1776, 1781

Congress of the Confederation 1781-1783, 1786-1787

US House of Representatives 1789–1797

US Secretary of State 1801–1809

President of the United States 1809-1817

On January 29, 1788, the New York Packet published an article by James Madison (Federalist 46), comparing the influence of the State and Federal governments.

As a starting point, Madison says:

I assume this position here as it respects the first, reserving the proofs for another place. The federal and State governments are in fact but different agents and trustees of the people, constituted with different powers, and designed for different purposes.

Madison's use of the term "the people" in the Second Amendment was deliberate, as powers ultimately belong to the people as a whole, but certain powers are entrusted to different levels of government. He continues to explain that he believes people will feel most attached to their state governments rather than the federal government.

They must be told that the ultimate authority, wherever the derivative may be found, resides in the people alone, and that it will not depend merely on the comparative ambition or address of the different governments, whether either, or which of them, will be able to enlarge its sphere of jurisdiction at the expense of the other. Truth, no less than decency, requires that the event in every case should be supposed to depend on the sentiments and sanction of their common constituents. Many considerations, besides those suggested on a former occasion, seem to place it beyond doubt that the first and most natural attachment of the people will be to the governments of their respective States.

You can see from the way he writes that he would be hesitant to say, "Each State in the union has a right to..." as he believed that the governments are simply agents and trustees of the people; thus, the power to make decisions ultimately rests with the people.

In discussing the benefits of state governments having authority over their militias, he says (in comparison to the European governments at the time):

It may well be doubted, whether a militia thus circumstanced could ever be conquered by such a proportion of regular troops. Those who are best acquainted with the last successful resistance of this country against the British arms, will be most inclined to deny the possibility of it. Besides the advantage of being armed, which the Americans possess over the people of almost every other nation, the existence of subordinate governments, to which the people are attached, and by which the militia officers are appointed, forms a barrier against the enterprises of ambition, more insurmountable than any which a simple government of any form can admit of. Notwithstanding the military establishments in the several kingdoms of Europe, which are carried as far as the public resources will bear, the governments are afraid to trust the people with arms. And it is not certain, that with this aid alone they would not be able to shake off their yokes. But were the people to possess the additional advantages of local governments chosen by themselves, who could collect the national will and direct the national force, and of officers appointed out of the militia, by these governments, and attached both to them and to the militia, it may be affirmed with the greatest assurance, that the throne of every tyranny in Europe would be speedily overturned in spite of the legions which surround it.

In this text, Madison mentions that Americans possess the ability to arm themselves. Notice that he doesn't say it in an "oh, we must protect this" type of tone. Instead, he says it as a matter of fact, as if it should simply be assumed. He also refers to the British troops that would face off against the American militia as "British Arms" – he's not just talking about British guns there, but the uniformed military units themselves.

Between 1787 and 1788 several state conventions were held to debate the adoption of the Federal Constitution. The US Constitution had been introduced, but no amendments yet existed. At each of these debates, the attendees discussed what changes would be needed to convince everyone there to adopt it. This is what led to the writing of the Bill of Rights, including the Second Amendment.

In Pennsylvania, the dissenting minority (Anti-Federalists) proposed a list of 14 propositions. Number seven was about the right to bear arms:

7. That the people have a right to bear arms for the defense of themselves and their own state, or the United States, or for the purpose of killing game; and no law shall be passed for disarming the people or any of them, unless for crimes committed, or real danger of public injury from individuals; and as standing armies in the time of peace are dangerous to liberty, they ought not to be kept up; and that the military shall be kept under strict subordination to and be governed by the civil powers.

This version is very different from the wording of the Second Amendment that was adopted, it did leave room for gun regulations if crimes were committed or if there was a real danger of public injury from individuals.

One proposed amendment by the people of New Hampshire was directly about gun ownership:

XII. Congress shall never disarm any citizen, unless such as are or have been in actual rebellion.

While this proposal was most certainly about gun ownership, it bears no similarity to the wording of the Second Amendment.

The Constitution was ratified in New York on July 26, 1788. A delegate from New York said, "*We, the delegates of the people of the state of New York, duly elected and met in Convention, having maturely considered the Constitution for the United States of America, agreed to on the 17th day of September*" ... "*Do declare and make known, -* " ... "*That the people have a right to keep and bear arms; that a well-regulated militia, including the body of the people capable of bearing arms, is the proper, natural, and safe defence of a free state.*" And "*That the Militia should not be subject to Martial Law except in time of War, Rebellion or Insurrection. That standing Armies in time of Peace are dangerous to Liberty, and ought not to be kept up, except in Cases of necessity; and that at all times, the Military should be under strict Subordination to the civil Power.*"

When the delegates from Rhode Island agreed to the US Constitution, they proposed amendments by saying they, "*do declare and make known –*"

XVII. *That the people have a right to keep and bear arms; that a well-regulated militia, including the body of the people capable of bearing arms, is the proper, natural, and safe defence of a free state; that the militia shall not be subject to martial law, except in time of war, rebellion, or insurrection; that standing armies, in time of peace, are dangerous to liberty, and ought not to be kept up, except in cases of necessity; and that, at all times, the military should be under strict subordination to the civil power; that, in time of peace, no soldier ought to be quartered in any house without the consent of the owner, and in time of war only by the civil magistrates, in such manner as the law directs.*

XVIII. *That any person religiously scrupulous of bearing arms ought to be exempted upon payment of an equivalent to employ another to bear arms in his stead.*

From the convention in Virginia, they proposed twenty amendments. Number Seventeen reads:

17th. That the people have a right to keep and bear arms; that a well-regulated militia, composed of the body of the people trained to arms, is the proper, natural, and safe defence of a free state; that standing armies, in time of peace, are dangerous to liberty, and therefore ought to be avoided, as far as the circumstances and protection of the community will admit; and that, in all cases, the military should be under strict subordination to, and governed by, the civil power.

Again, the military should be under strict subordination to, and governed by, the civil power – the people.

In the second set of twenty amendments proposed that day was another amendment resembling what would become the Second Amendment:

11th. That each state respectively shall have the power to provide for organizing, arming, and disciplining its own militia, whensoever Congress shall omit or neglect to provide for the same. That the militia shall not be subject to martial law, except when in actual service, in time of war, invasion, or rebellion; and when not in the actual service of the United States, shall be subject only to such fines, penalties, and punishments, as shall be directed or inflicted by the laws of its own state.

This version makes a more direct case that the States should have power over the militia rather than the Federal Government. There was a lot of debate over what would become the Second Amendment. Still, the discussion was focused on State power vs. Federal power over the militia, not if individuals should be able to have a protected right to own a firearm for use outside the scope of a militia.

Similar versions were introduced in the various debates in

several states over the US Constitution and the Bill of Rights.

Patrick Henry

Virginia House of Burgesses 1765-1768, 1769-1776

Virginia House of Delegates 1779-1784, 1787-1790, 1799

Continental Congress 1774-1775

Governor of Virginia 1784-1786, 1776-1779

On the topic of the militia, Anti-Federalist Patrick Henry said, *"Have we the means of resisting disciplined armies, when our only defence, the militia, is put in the hands of Congress?"* He went on to say:

Let me here call your attention to that part which gives the Congress power "to provide for organizing, arming, and disciplining the militia, and for governing such part of them as may be employed in the service of the United States-reserving to the states, respectively, the appointment of the officers, and the authority of training the militia according to the discipline prescribed by Congress." By this, sir, you see that their control over our last and best defence is unlimited. If they neglect or refuse to discipline or arm our militia, they will be useless: the states can do neither-this power being exclusively given to Congress. The power of appointing officers over men not disciplined or armed is ridiculous; so that this pretended little remains of power left to the states may, at the pleasure of Congress, be rendered nugatory. Our situation will be deplorable indeed: nor can we ever expect to get this government amended, since I have already shown that a very small minority may prevent it, and that small minority interested in the continuance of the oppression. Will the oppressor let go the oppressed? Was there ever an instance? Can the annals of mankind exhibit one single example where rulers overcharged with power willingly let go the oppressed, though solicited and requested most earnestly? The application for amendments will therefore be fruitless. Sometimes, the oppressed have got loose by one of those bloody struggles that desolate a country; but a willing relinquishment of power is one of those things which human nature never was, nor ever will be, capable of.

Patrick Henry's point was that Article 1 Section 8 was insufficient in assuring states that they could have control over their militias and that Congress could render the state militia meaningless by failing to discipline or arm them. He called the powers granted to the States in Article 1 Section 8 *"pretended little remains of power left to the states."*-Saying that the States required more power over their militias. If it were not clear that he was talking about the interest of the States, he said explicitly, *"On this occasion, I conceived myself bound to attend strictly to the interest of the state, and I thought her dearest rights at stake."*

George Mason had the same concern:

Under various pretences, Congress may neglect to provide for arming and disciplining the militia; and the state governments cannot do it, for Congress has an exclusive right to arm them, &c. Here is a line of division drawn between them-the state and general governments. The power over the militia is divided between them. The national government has an exclusive right to provide for arming, organizing, and disciplining the militia, and for governing such part of them as may be employed in the service of the United States. The state governments have the power of appointing the officers, and of training the militia, according to the discipline prescribed by Congress, if they should think proper to prescribe any. Should the national government wish to render the militia useless, they may neglect them, and let them perish, in order to have a pretence of establishing a standing army.

While debating what would become the Second Amendment,

the Framers were having a discussion about State vs. National government powers over the militia. The Anti-Federalists were advocating for State rights, not individual gun ownership rights.

Richard Henry Lee

Virginia House of Burgesses 1758-1776

Congress of the Confederation 1784-1787

President of the Congress of the Confederation 1784-1785

United States Senator 1789-1792

President pro tem of the US Senate 1792

Many of the Federalists agreed with Alexander Hamilton that the argument had no merit. Richard Henry Lee said:

I cannot understand the implication of the honorable gentleman, that, because Congress may arm the militia, the states cannot do it: nor do I understand the reverse of the proposition. The states are, by no part of the plan before you, precluded from arming and disciplining the militia, should Congress neglect it.

The Anti-Federalists stood their ground on this issue, and George Mason worded their request best when he said:

I stand on the general principles of freedom, whereon I dare to meet any one. I wish that, in case the general government should neglect to arm and discipline the militia, there should be an express declaration that the state governments might arm and discipline them. With this single exception, I would agree to this part, as I am conscious the government ought to have the power.

This is worth repeating "there should be an express declaration that the state governments might arm and discipline them," that declaration is the Second Amendment.

Another theme to pay attention to is the stress the Framers put on military discipline. They weren't simply talking about the militia being armed, they were talking about the militia being trained in the art of war and being effective on the battlefield.

James Wilson

Continental Congress 1775-1777

Supreme Court of the United States 1789-1798

James Wilson made the point about how a well-regulated militia can be a "bulwark of internal strength":

I believe any gentleman, who possesses military experience, will inform you that men without a uniformity of arms, accoutrements, and discipline, are no more than a mob in a camp; that, in the field, instead of assisting, they interfere with one another. If a soldier drops his musket, and his companion, unfurnished with one, takes it up, it is of no service, because his cartridges do not fit it. By means of this system, a uniformity of arms and discipline will prevail throughout the United States.

I really expected that, for this part of the system at least, the framers of it would have received plaudits instead of censures, as they here discover a strong anxiety to have this body put upon an effective footing, and thereby, in a great measure, to supersede the necessity of raising or keeping up standing armies.

The militia formed under this system, and trained by the several states, will be such a bulwark of internal strength, as to prevent the attacks of foreign enemies. I have been told that, about the year 1744, an attack was intended by France upon Massachusetts Bay, but was given up on reading the militia law of the province.

If a single state could deter an enemy from such attempts, what influence will the proposed arrangement have upon the different powers of Europe?

In every point of view, this regulation is calculated to produce good effects. How powerful and respectable must the body of militia appear under general and uniform regulations!

George Mason weighed in on this point as well (Yeomanry are middle class):

No man has a greater regard for the military gentlemen than I have. I admire their intrepidity, perseverance, and valor. But when once a standing army is established in any country, the people lose their liberty. When, against a regular and disciplined army, yeomanry are the only defence,-yeomanry, unskilful and unarmed,- what chance is there for preserving freedom?

James Madison, Alexander Hamilton, and several others made the case that militias should, except in times of federal need, report to the people of the State over the Federal Government.

James Madison explained the importance of a federal government built from the bottom up rather than the top down so that local governments collect the national will and direct the national force rather than a top-down authority which can result in tyranny. Thus, the Federal Government should not be taking away the authority over the armed militia from the people of a state.

When James Madison gave his speech to Congress, introducing the Bill of Rights, he didn't single out the Second Amendment in his commentary, but he did make a distinction between natural rights and rights resulting from a social compact, such as trial by jury.

In some instances they assert those rights which are exercised by the people in forming and establishing a plan of Government. In other instances, they specify those rights which are retained when particular powers are given up to be exercised by the Legislature. In other instances, they specify positive rights, which may seem to result from the nature of the compact. Trial by jury cannot be considered as a natural right, but a right resulting from a social compact, which regulates the action of the community, but is as essential to secure the liberty of the people as any one of the pre-existent rights of nature. In other instances, they lay down dogmatic maxims with respect to the construction of the Government; declaring that the Legislative, Executive, and Judicial branches, shall be kept separate and distinct. Perhaps the best way of securing this in practice is, to provide such checks as will prevent the encroachment of the one upon the other.

When James Madison proposed the Bill of Rights, a collection of an initial seventeen articles condensed down to 12 articles (by combining some of them), to the House of Representatives on June 8, 1789 – he streamlined the Second Amendment into one sentence. The version of the Second Amendment he proposed was:

The right of the people to keep and bear arms shall not be infringed; a well armed and well regulated militia being the best security of a free country: but no person religiously scrupulous of bearing arms shall be compelled to render military service in person.

A semicolon is often used to separate independent clauses closely related in meaning. The right of the people to keep and bear arms means that the people can't be denied a well-armed and well-regulated militia. You can also see the concern that the amendment might lead to people being forced to take up arms who may have religious objections — in the context of military service.

Our first president, George Washington, had much to say on

the topic as well. In the first State of the Union speech, he said in his own words how important the well-regulated militia the Second Amendment protects is:

A free people ought not only to be armed, but disciplined; to which end a uniform and well-digested plan is requisite; and their safety and interest require that they should promote such manufactories as tend to render them independent of others for essential, particularly military, supplies.

The proper establishment of the troops which may be deemed indispensable will be entitled to mature consideration. In the arrangements which may be made respecting it it will be of importance to conciliate the comfortable support of the officers and soldiers with a due regard to economy.

George Washington had long been a proponent for bringing more uniform training and discipline to the militia of each independent State so that when called together they would be more formidable than some of the militiamen he had seen.

Article the fourth, US Bill of Rights, which reads "Article the fourth... A well regulated Militia, being necessary to the security of a free State, the right of the people to keep and bear Arms, shall not be infringed."

The Supreme Court elaborates

Joseph Story

US House of Representatives 1808-1809

Supreme Court of the United States 1811-1845

As the Supreme Court was created to be the authority on interpreting the US Constitution, several Supreme Court Justices have written about the US Constitution and how to properly interpret it. When James Madison was President, he appointed Justice Joseph Story to the Supreme Court in 1812. Justice Story wrote Commentaries on the Constitution of the United States. On the Second Amendment, he wrote:

Sec. 1889. The next amendment is: "A well regulated militia being necessary to the security of a free state, the right of the people to keep and bear arms shall not be infringed."

Sec. 1890. The importance of this article will scarcely be doubted by any persons, who have duly reflected upon the subject. The militia is the natural defence of a free country against sudden foreign invasions, domestic insurrections, and domestic usurpations of power by rulers. It is against sound policy for a free people to keep up large military establishments and standing armies in time of peace, both from the enormous expenses, with which they are attended, and the facile means, which they afford to ambitious and unprincipled rulers, to subvert the government, or trample upon the rights of the people. The right of the citizens to keep and bear arms has justly been considered, as the palladium of the liberties of a republic; since it offers a strong moral check against the usurpation and arbitrary power of rulers; and will generally, even if these are successful in the first instance, enable the people to resist and triumph over them. And yet, though this truth would seem so clear, and the importance of a well regulated militia would seem so undeniable, it cannot be disguised, that among the American people there is a growing indifference to any system of militia discipline, and a strong disposition, from a sense of its burdens, to be rid of all regulations. How it is practicable to keep the people duly armed without some organization, it is difficult to see. There is certainly no small danger, that indifference may lead to disgust, and disgust to contempt; and thus gradually undermine all the protection intended by this clause of our national bill of rights.

Justice Story is talking about the militia while covering the Second Amendment, and the importance of its existence which he felt people were starting to take for granted (becoming indifferent to). He also discusses the "strong moral check" of having a strong militia over a strong standing army. He is referring to the likelihood of someone disobeying an order they find unethical. That's how we can prevent a tyrannical government, by not providing the want-to-be tyrants with a military force that will follow tyrannical orders without question. For example, a soldier may be willing to follow an order to suppress innocent people far from home but would be less willing to follow an order to suppress their family, neighbor, or co-worker.

Before moving on to providing commentary about a different amendment, Justice Story points out that the provision mentioned in the English Bill of Rights is "more nominal than real."

Sec. 1891. A similar provision in favour of protestants (for to them it is confined) is to be found in the bill of rights of 1688, it being declared, "that the subjects, which are protestants, may have arms for their defence suitable to their condition, and as allowed by law." But under various pretences the effect of this provision has been greatly narrowed; and it is at present in England more nominal than real, as a defensive privilege.

Thomas Cooley

Michigan Supreme Court 1858-1864

Supreme Court of the United States 1864-1885

Courtesy The
Michigan Supreme Court
Historical Society

Justice Thomas Cooley also wrote extensively about the US Constitution. In <u>The General Principles of Constitutional Law In The United States of America</u>, he stated:

Section IV.--The Right to Keep and Bear Arms

The Constitution.--By the second amendment to the Constitution it is declared that, 'a well-regulated militia being necessary to the security of a free state, the right of the people to keep and bear arms shall not be infringed.'

The amendment, like most other provisions in the Constitutions, has a history. It was adopted with some modification and enlargement from the English Bill of Rights of 1688, where it stood as a protest against arbitrary action of the overturned dynasty in disarming the people, and as a pledge of the new rulers that this tyrannical action should cease. The right declared was meant to be a strong moral check against the usurpation and arbitrary power of rulers, and as a necessary and efficient means of regaining rights when temporarily overturned by usurpation.

The Right is General.--It might be supposed from the phraseology of this provision that the right to keep and bear arms was only guaranteed to the militia; but this would be an interpretation not warranted by the intent. The militia, as has been elsewhere explained, consists of those persons who, under the law, are liable to the performance of military duty, and are officered and enrolled for service when called upon. But the law may make provision for the enrolment of all who are fit to perform military duty, or of a small number only, or it may wholly omit to make any provision at all; and if the right were limited to those enrolled, the purpose of this guaranty might be defeated altogether by the action or neglect to act of the government it was meant to hold in check. The meaning of the provision undoubtedly is, that the people, from whom the militia must be taken, shall have the right to keep and bear arms; and they need no permission or regulation of law for the purpose. But this enables the government to have a well-regulated militia; for to bear arms implies something more than the mere keeping; it implies the learning to handle and use them in a way that makes those who keep them ready for their efficient use; in other words, it implies the right to meet for voluntary discipline in arms, observing in doing so the laws of public order.

Standing Army.--A further purpose of this amendment is, to preclude any necessity or reasonable excuse for keeping up a standing army. A standing army is condemned by the traditions and sentiments of the people, as being as dangerous to the liberties of the people as the general preparation of the people for the defence of their institutions with arms is preservative of them.

What Arms may be kept.--The arms intended by the Constitution are such as are suitable for the general defence of the community against invasion or oppression, and the secret carrying of those suited merely to deadly individual encounters may be prohibited.

His interpretation echoes Justice Story's, including the moral check.

The right being general doesn't always offer clarity on modern debates about the intentions of the Second Amendment, but the fact that the meaning of "keep and bear arms" is about much more than simply keeping arms is. As Justice Cooley says, it's also about discipline in arms – being prepared to fight and be effective in a military pursuit. What he is clarifying is that the Second Amendment doesn't mean only militia members can own arms, it's more generalized that that, but he doesn't at any point say that the Second Amendment is about everyone being able to own arms, he says it instead "implies the right to meet for voluntary discipline in arms, observing in doing so the laws of public order".

The Collective Rights Theory

The Collective Rights Theory is the interpretation that the Second Amendment exists to say that the Federal Government can't prevent states from having a well-regulated armed militia, and states are required to maintain a well-regulated armed militia. Like the right to a trial by jury, it is a right resulting from a social compact. It just says that any individual right to a firearm not related to a well-regulated militia for the security of a free State is outside the amendment's scope. The interpretation doesn't say that people cannot own guns individually. It is recognized by those who interpret the Second Amendment under The Collective Rights Theory that the Founders of the United States fully expected free men to have the ability to own personal arms outside the scope of a militia. Building on the established Constitutional purpose of a militia in Article 1 Section 8 to "execute the Laws" and "suppress Insurrections and repel Invasions." The Second Amendment is about a state's ability to deploy its organized militia, not the absolute right of anyone in the unorganized militia to own a firearm. In other words, it isn't that the right described in the Second Amendment is a collective right; it is that it is achieved collectively: like our individual right to a trial jury if we are charged with a crime. With the context above, let's review the final wording of the Second Amendment:

A well regulated Militia, being necessary to the security of a free State, the right of the people to keep and bear Arms, shall not be infringed.

A misconception about The Collective Rights Theory is that it is about disarming people. The framers assumed that the American people, in general, would have and maintain the ability to arm themselves. The idea that The Collective Rights

Theory would lead to all guns being taken away from law-abiding citizens is a slippery slope fallacy. While the Second Amendment, under The Collective Rights Theory, would not prevent the regulation of firearms, it wouldn't guarantee it either. It still serves as a federal hindrance, as any federal law that limits access to firearms cannot do so to the point of infringing upon a state's right to an armed militia. Additionally, many state constitutions include an individual right to bear arms.

Article 1 Section 8 of the US Constitution also provides a limitation on the State governments, as the Second Amendment places a limitation on the Federal Government. If Congress has the power to call forth the Militia at a federal level, then the States cannot disarm the people to the point of Congress being unable to do so.

To understand the sentence structure of the Second Amendment, we can also try changing the sentence to be about Libraries instead of Militias and Books instead of Arms:

A well-stocked Library, being necessary to the education of a free State, the right of the people to have access to books, shall not be infringed.

If this were an amendment in the US Constitution, it wouldn't ban the personal ownership of books; it would simply protect the ability for people to go to libraries.

The right to bear arms mentioned in the Second Amendment isn't comparable to personal book ownership. It's comparable to the right to have a well-stocked library because the right to keep and bear arms, in the Second Amendment, explicitly talks about assembling armed people for a military purpose.

Bearing arms could also mean showing your Coat of Arms – in other words, a military display of loyalty. "The right to keep and bear arms" could be referencing more than simply 'being armed" but being in uniform. In England, there is "The Law of

Arms," which covers the rules of who may bear the arms of their family. These cadency marks would be placed on items such as shields and would typically only pass down to male heirs unless there were no male heirs. In the American Revolution, soldiers would wear a waistcoat and a wool regimental coat. The coats had various lapels and cuffs called "facings." Unlike a Coat of Arms, these colors typically didn't signify family relationships; instead, they distinguished between ranks, states, or even what unit a soldier was a part of. The color of the Continental Army uniforms varied a bit. A blue coat with white pants was common, but material shortages and supply line difficulties made consistency difficult. Many militiamen wore their personal civilian clothing but often still wore specific hats or colors to display rank. In contrast, the British soldiers often wore bright red coats, leading to the nickname "The Redcoats."

In any case, "the right to keep and bear arms" is to assemble a military unit from the people. The Tennessee Supreme Court said in 1840, "A man in the pursuit of deer, elk, and buffaloes might carry his rifle every day for forty years, and yet it would never be said of him that he had borne arms; much less could it be said that a private citizen bears arms because he has a dirk or pistol concealed under his clothes, or a spear in a cane."

> National Guardsmen are:
> Citizens most of the time,
> Soldiers some of the time,
> Patriots all of the time.
>
> Brigadier General James Drain
> Washington National Guard
> 1928

Photo from the National Guard Memorial Museum in Washington D.C.

The Individual Rights Theory

To reach the interpretation we call The Individual Rights Theory, one must split the emphasis of the amendment into two completely separate thoughts or clauses.

The prefatory clause:

A well regulated Militia, being necessary to the security of a free State

The operative clause:

the right of the people to keep and bear Arms shall not be infringed

While The Collective Rights Theory emphasizes the important context the prefatory clause provides (that the amendment exists to protect the states in their authority to maintain well-organized militias) and says that the Second Amendment protects a right resulting from a social compact, The Individual Rights Theory only focuses on the operative clause and the idea that the Second Amendment merely talks about a natural right that exists outside of government (that individuals are protected in their ability to arm themselves).

In other words, one doesn't have to be a member of an organized militia to maintain a constitutional right to own a firearm, just the unorganized militia (men 17–45 according to 10 U.S. Code § 246). The strictest form of this interpretation makes most gun control laws unconstitutional.

Alternatively, many who agree with The Individual Rights Theory claim that everyone capable of arming themselves is part of the militia.

The partial quote from George Mason often repeated is, "*Who are the militia? They consist now of the whole people, except a few public officers."* However, he was remarking on the state of the nation after the American Revolution; he wasn't claiming that the militia mentioned in the Constitution would be made up of the entire population of the United States. Here's a more extended passage that provides context to the quote:

> *I ask, Who are the militia? They consist now of the whole people, except a few public officers. But I cannot say who will be the militia of the future day. If that paper on the table gets no alteration, the militia of the future day may not consist of all classes, high and low, and rich and poor; but they may be confined to the lower and middle classes of the people, granting exclusion to the higher classes of the people. If we should ever see that day, the most ignominious punishments and heavy fines may be expected. Under the present government, all ranks of people are subject to militia duty. Under such a full and equal representation as ours, there can be no ignominious punishment inflicted. But under this national, or rather consolidated government, the case will be different. The representation being so small and inadequate, they will have no fellow-feeling for the people. They may discriminate people in their own predicament, and exempt from duty all the officers and lowest creatures of the national government. If there were a more particular definition of their powers, and a clause exempting the militia from martial law except when in actual service, and from fines and punishments of an unusual nature, then we might expect that the militia would be what they are. But, if this be not the case, we cannot say how long all classes of people will be included in the militia.*

George Mason wasn't saying that everyone is "the militia" he was speaking of an uncertain future as to who future militia members may be and telling those who were framing the Bill of Rights that steps should be taken to ensure that the United States doesn't become a class-based system where only the lower classes will be forced into militia duty.

A similar quote favored by those who support the Individual

Rights Theory is by Tench Coxe, who said:

The power of the sword, say the minority... is in the hands of Congress. My friends and countrymen, it is not so, for The powers of the sword are in the hands of the yeomanry of America from sixteen to sixty. The militia of these free commonwealths, entitled and accustomed to their arms, when compared with any possible army, must be tremendous and irresistible. Who are the militia? Are they not ourselves? Is it feared, then, that we shall turn our arms each man against his own bosom. Congress has no power to disarm the militia. Their swords and every terrible implement of the soldier are the birthright of Americans. The unlimited power of the sword is not in the hands of either the federal or state governments but where, I trust in God, it will always remain, in the hands of the people.

Tench Coxe

Continental Congress 1788

Assistant Secretary of the Treasury 1789-1792

Courtesy
The New York
Public Library

Tench Coxe was a politician from Pennsylvania, and later the assistant secretary of the Treasury under Alexander Hamilton. He was a firm believer in the individual right to gun ownership, and the responsibility to rebel against a tyrannical government (such as Great Britain of the time). Coxe had been a private in the Pennsylvania militia before becoming an international merchant, running the company Coxe & Frazier, which dealt in various commodities, including the sale of firearms. Coxe & Frazier sold arms to state and local militias and also made them available for private purchase. The sale of arms to militias and the army often overwhelmed his offices. This does not invalidate any of the Tench Coxe quotes, but it should be taken into context that he didn't just represent an individual who wanted personal gun rights, he was also representing the gun industry as he personally profited from increased gun and ammo sales.

David I. Caplan was one of the most outspoken advocates for The Independent Rights Theory, publishing three articles on the topic from 1976 to 1982, such as Gun Control Jeopardizes All Our Constitutional Rights and Handgun Control: Constitutional or Unconstitutional - A Reply to Mayor Jackson and Restoring the Balance – The Second Amendment Revisited. He was a lawyer and the chief counsel of the Federation of Greater New York Rifle and Pistol Clubs Inc.

Caplan put forth that the Second Amendment had two goals, both collective and individual defense. He argued that the unorganized militia (as per 10 U.S. Code § 246) doesn't make sense unless everyone in that category (able-bodies males at least 17 years of age, etc.) can own a gun before being called into service. Most of his arguments, like that one, are from the stance of "Oh, we should have guns; therefore, that's what the Second Amendment is about," however the only way he ever linked the right to individual defense is through a loose association of the fact that free men of the time period were expected to be able to own arms.

In framing The Collective Rights Theory, Caplan would describe it as if it excluded individual rights:

One of the favorite arguments disparaging the Second Amendment is that "the right of the people to keep and bear arms" is merely a collective right referring only to the people collectively as a common body.

And was thus in conflict with other amendments which speak of individual rights:

Moreover, those who think that "the right of the people to keep and bear arms refers only to a collective right confront a serious threshold problem in their interpretation of the First and Fourth Amendments in our Bill of Rights

However, those who support The Collective Rights Theory interpretation recognize that the Second Amendment protects an "individual" right, which isn't the point of contention. The difference is what that individual right is. Is it the right to be armed outside the scope of a militia for personal defense, or is it the right of the people to come together and bear arms through a well-regulated militia for the common defense? Perhaps the fact that Caplan couldn't disprove the latter is why he claimed that the Second Amendment protects both.

Another common argument presented to support The Individual Rights Theory is that militia members were expected to provide their own guns in colonial times, and according to the Militia Acts of 1792, which stated:

That the commissioned Officers shall severally be armed with a sword or hanger, and espontoon; and that from and after five years from the passing of this Act, all muskets from arming the militia as is herein required, shall be of bores sufficient for balls of the eighteenth part of a pound; and every citizen so enrolled, and providing himself with the arms, ammunition and accoutrements, required as aforesaid, shall hold the same exempted from all suits, distresses, executions or sales, for debt or for the payment of taxes.

Since a law from 1792 said that the militia members must provide themselves with arms, they theorize that the Second Amendment ratified in 1791 meant that militia members must provide themselves with arms too. It is not a logical comparison because the Second Amendment doesn't quantify where the arms need to come from. Article 1 Section 8 clearly says that

Congress has the power (not the mandate) to provide for the militia. The Militia Acts of 1792 were later replaced by laws that removed this requirement for militia members to provide their own arms, so mentioning that militia members once had this requirement is merely a historical reference that has no bearing on current law or interpretations of the Second Amendment.

Another idea that supporters of The Independent Rights Theory tend to hold onto is that the Federalists wanted the government to have the power over arms and standing armies, and the Anti-Federalists wanted the Constitution to say that everyone could own a gun without infringement, even when not associated with a militia. This entire argument is false. In reality, none of the Framers liked the idea of a standing army, but overall, they believed it was necessary. To understand that, one need only read Alexander Hamilton's and James Madison's Federalist Papers. The Second Amendment was also not introduced to counter the standing army; that is not what the Anti-Federalists like George Mason and Patrick Henry were arguing against. The actual arguments were over the role the militia would play in the new government and the balance of power the general (federal) government would have over the militia versus the state government's power over the militia. It was not so extreme that any party felt that the militia should wholly report to one or the other; it was closer to if they were saying it should be 60/40 one way or 40/60 the other way. The Federalists believed that a strong general government was needed, and the Anti-Federalists believed that strong State governments were required. Both sides saw the importance of having both General and State governments.

Despite the lack of evidence from the US Constitution, the words of the framers, or Supreme Court Cases before 2008, the Individual Rights Theory has been strongly backed by gun manufacturers and gun lobby groups, such as the National Rifle Association (NRA), and a strong following within the Federalist Society – which is an organization of primarily conservative lawyers and judges.

Warren Burger

US Court of Appeals for D.C. Circuit
1956-1969

Supreme Court of the United States
1969-1986

The bias of those supporting the Individual Rights Theory led (conservative) Supreme Court Justice Warren Burger to say in a PBS interview in 1991, "*The gun lobby's interpretation of the Second Amendment is one of the greatest pieces of fraud, I repeat the word fraud, on the American people by special interest groups that I have ever seen in my lifetime.*" In an article he wrote for the Associate Press about the Bill of Rights that same year, he said "*the real purpose of the Second Amendment was to ensure that state armies, the militia, would be maintained for the defense of the state*" and "*The very language of the Second Amendment refutes any argument that it was intended to guarantee every citizen an unfettered right to any kind of weapon he or she desires.*"

What both theories have in common

Regardless of which of these two interpretations you believe is correct, they have some things in common.

They both only limit the government's actions.

They both say the Federal Government can't completely disarm the people.

They can both be interpreted as the Second Amendment protecting an individual right.

Linguistics

The phrasing of the Second Amendment is highly debated, with some saying that it is phrased poorly, or is messy, and others who claim it was perfect grammar for the time. This leads to many arguments about the meaning of the Second Amendment being about the other party "rewriting it" as you have to "rewrite it" to get across how you interpret it. This method is employed throughout this book to distinguish the different interpretations.

Some people think that the Second Amendment reads like this: "The individual rights of the people to have weapons or armor and carry weapons for offense or defense just in case of conflict, shall not be abridged — just in case properly disciplined and trained males physically capable of acting in concert for the common defense are needed for any reason for a free country or polity."

While others think it reads like this: "A militia trained by the States according to the discipline prescribed by Congress, being necessary for a State to execute the law, repel invasions, and suppress insurrections; the right of the people to a well-regulated State militia, shall not be infringed."

The point is that due to the way it's phrased, it's not clear to everyone what the sentence meant then, in relation to today's English.

One of the issues is that today we don't often start a clause with the word "being". "This information being also this information" is unfamiliar territory, at least in spoken English. What this type of clause usually does is provide additional context. "Being from Louisiana, I like spicy foods." That I am from Louisiana and that I like spicy foods are two distinct facts, but there's typically a connection because Louisiana is known for spicy foods. In the Second Amendment it says "A well regulated Militia" then "being necessary to the security of a free state" is adding the context that the Militia is needed for a specific purpose, the security of a free state. Both of these phrases, however, are just a quick reference to what's in Article 1 Section 8, which explains how the Militia will be kept well regulated and explains why it is necessary. The best way to deal with this section of the Second Amendment is to understand that it is there to provide context for the rest of the sentence.

Linguistically, the most challenging part of the Second Amendment to reconcile is probably "the right of the people to keep and bear Arms." You can look up "to bear" in a dictionary and quickly find "to carry" but few cover what it means to "bear arms" as a whole, because dictionaries focus on single words not the meanings of phrases. From the time period there are several examples of "bear arms" or "bearing arms" being used within a military context, but there are also examples of it being used outside of a military context. Thus, the importance and understanding of context is the heart of most Second Amendment discussions.

Likewise, the meaning of "Keep... arms" is a disputed point, it has fewer historical references than "bear arms" and how it is interpreted has the greatest impact on the Second Amendment implications for today. Does it mean that everyone has the individual right to keep arms? Or does it mean that the people, collectively, have the right to have an armed militia? When we look at it through the lens of corpus-linguistics (a method for studying authentic texts, in this case writings from the time period) we find that half of the times "keep...arms" was used, it was in the scope of a military context, a quarter of the times they were talking about private ownership, and the remaining references were unclear.

While the phrase "the right of the people" is not directly

disputed among Supreme Court Justices, who have said that the Second Amendment refers to an individual right, it is still a phrase often compared to how "the people" is used in other Amendments. Within the First Amendment it says "right of the people peaceably to assemble," so does this mean that people have the individual right to assemble or the collective right to assemble? The answer is both. We each have the individual right to assemble, but we can't assemble with other people unless there's other people assembling with us. The Fourth Amendment provides a slightly different context, however, as it says "The right of the people to be secure in their persons, houses, papers, and effects, against unreasonable searches and seizures, shall not be violated," again if we ask does this mean individually or collectively – it means both. You in your house, even if you live alone, have a Fourth Amendment right to be secure in your home, just as members of a Church have a right to have their church being secure against unreasonable search and seizure. Some have argued that the individual vs collective nature of the Second Amendment relates to if one has to participate in some corporate body in order to exercise that right, but the only way to get there is to first convince yourself that the topic is personal gun ownership rather than access to a state militia. Within the scope of how Supreme Court Justices have viewed the Second Amendment, no one has ever said that the Second Amendment means that only those in a state militia can own firearms, so that argument has less to do with linguistics and is more about building a straw man argument.

The last phrase "shall not be infringed" is not something that linguistics tells us much about, again we need to look at context. The Bill of Rights was written to limit the powers of Congress. Thus, whatever right is being discussed, it is Congress the Second Amendment is protecting it from. Congress can't make any law which would infringe upon the rights described in the Second Amendment.

In the end trying to understand each section of the Second

Amendment strictly through linguistics may be less useful than focusing on the context and intent of the Framers, as language changes over time and even if we take historical use into account the same phrases were used in multiple ways.

Common Arguments

"The people" has the same meaning throughout the Constitution.

The phrase "the people" appears nine times in the Constitution and its Amendments. It starts with "We the People of the United States" set out to accomplish something collectively. Then it says that we collectively choose people for the House of Representatives. The First Amendment says "The people" have the right to assemble; clearly, every individual has the right to assemble, but we can't assemble unless we do so collectively with at least one other person. Then it is used in the Second Amendment, where we are either talking about the people of a state collectively having a right to an armed state militia or individually having a right to bear arms. The Fourth Amendment says "in their persons" after "the people"; thus, the context is provided to understand that we are talking about people individually. The Ninth and Tenth Amendments are catch-alls; the Ninth Amendment could be read either way, depending on the situation. The Tenth lists the States and "the people" separately — providing enough context to imply that individual rights are covered. The Seventeenth Amendment talks about the people electing Senators and filling vacancies, so it uses the term collectively (individually, we have the right to vote, collectively, we have the right to select public officials through elections.) The phrase, "the people" means "a collection of human beings," so it is a collective term by default. To determine if it is being used to describe everyone in that collection individually or some action that the collection does together, we need to examine the context of the sentence where the term is used.

Everything in The Bill of Rights applies to individual rights

There were originally 17 Articles in The Bill of Rights. Only twelve of them made it out of the Senate as recommended Amendments. The first one was about how many people should be in Congress. The second one was, "*No law varying the compensation to the members of Congress shall take effect, until an election of representatives shall have intervened.*" Eventually, this became the 27th Amendment, which is not about individual rights. It's a limitation on Congress, so they can't give themselves a raise during a term. The sixteenth of the draft articles was "*The powers delegated by the constitution to the government of the United States, shall be exercised as therein appropriated, so that the legislative shall never exercise the powers vested in the executive or judicial; nor the executive the powers vested in the legislative or judicial; nor the judicial the powers vested in the legislative or executive.*" Thus, it was about keeping the separation of powers between branches intact, not about individual rights. Even if you look at the Tenth Amendment, which did make it into the approved Bill of Rights, it says, "*The powers not delegated to the United States by the Constitution, nor prohibited by it to the States, are reserved to the States respectively, or to the people.*" When it says "are reserved to the States respectively," that's not talking about individual rights. The Bill of Rights was written and introduced "*to prevent misconstruction or abuse of [the Constitution's] powers, that further declaratory and restrictive clauses should be added: And as extending the ground of public confidence in the Government, will best ensure the beneficent ends of its institution.*" The focus was on limitations on government power, not simply providing for individual rights.

Regardless of whether the Bill of Rights is limited to individual rights or not, the actual difference between The Individual Rights Theory and historical interpretations isn't if the right described in the Second Amendment can be described as one that is separately possessed and may be separately enforced, by each person on whom it is conferred – the difference is in what that right is. Is it the right to a well-regulated State Militia or the right to own firearms outside the scope of a Militia?

Well-regulated meant something other than regulated by the government

The word "regulate" is in the Constitution three times. Congress regulates commerce with foreign nations and regulates currency, and the Second Amendment talks about a well-regulated militia. Typically, when we think of rules and regulations, we are talking about laws; thus, regulating would be something Congress or State Legislatures do. In the Second Amendment, "well-regulated" refers to the state legislature putting rules and regulations in place for the militia to follow, such as Alexander Hamilton's suggestion that they be armed and then trained once or twice a year. Some will argue that it is a phrase that means something like "working as expected, calibrated correctly, normal, regular"; in other words, in effective shape to fight. However, the difference here is so subtle that it has little effect on the overall meaning of the Second Amendment; how could the people of a State ensure that a militia is in effective shape to fight if they never assemble?

Some have made the argument that "well regulated" simply means "in good working order" so if your gun is "in good working order" then it's "well regulated," however the Amendment says that it is the militia that's well-regulated, not the arms.

In the Second Amendment, well-regulated means that the State will train the militia according to discipline prescribed by Congress (Article 1 Section 8), armed (Second Amendment), and be assembled at least once or twice a year (Federalist 29).

The Second Amendment didn't create State Militias

This is true; State Militias existed before the US Constitution was ratified.

The Massachusetts National Guard is thus the oldest State Militia in the United States. It was organized in Massachusetts on December 13th, 1636. There were three regiments. The US Constitution wasn't signed until 1787.

When the Militia Act of 1792 was passed, all existing militia units were allowed to retain their "customary privileges." That provision was upheld in the Militia Act of 1903 and the National Defense Act of 1916.

What part of 'shall not be infringed' do you not understand?

The meaning of this phrase is not often debated. It is generally agreed upon that it refers to a limitation on the government.

The Second Amendment applies to the National Guard

The State Militias were named the National Guard in the Militia Act of 1903. The "well-regulated militias" in the Second Amendment are talking about the National Guard and any other organized Militia at the State Level (like a state Naval Militia). The National Guard is trained by the State according to the discipline prescribed by Congress, officers are appointed by the state, and they are assembled for drills one weekend a month and one two-week period a year. This does not mean that only members of the National Guard have the right to buy, keep, and carry weapons. The people of the state have a right to an armed and organized militia.

10 U.S. Code § 246 says:

The classes of the militia are—
(1)the organized militia, which consists of the National Guard and the Naval Militia; and
(2)the unorganized militia, which consists of the members of the militia who are not members of the National Guard or the Naval Militia.

The unorganized militia mentioned there is a foundation for State based conscription. Despite the fact that there hasn't been a state-level draft for hundreds of years, the foundation for that possibility is still there.

The Founding Fathers never meant that individuals should be armed

This point is both false and irrelevant to the Second Amendment. The Founding Fathers clearly expected that most free law-abiding men in the United States would have access to arms. However, just because they felt that most free law-abiding men should have access to guns, that doesn't mean that they opposed gun regulations (which existed at the time) or that they decided to make the Second Amendment about that.

The truth is that at the time gun regulations were a state and/or local government issue. They didn't restrict state and local governments from passing or keeping gun regulations any more than they restricted state and local governments from making regulations about motor vehicles, or horses and buggies.

The Second Amendment was to support slave owners

While the primary goal of the Second Amendment was to provide more power to the States over their militia as opposed to the Federal Government, and not anything to do with slavery, a slave uprising was considered a type of insurrection.

During the Virginia Debates over the Adoption of the Federal Constitution, George Nicholas said:

Another worthy member says there is no power in the states to quell an insurrection of slaves. Have they it now? If they have, does the Constitution take it away? If it does, it must be in one of the three clauses which have been mentioned by the worthy member. The first clause gives the general government power to call them out when necessary. Does this take it away from the states? No. But it gives an additional security; for, besides the power in the state governments to use their own militia, it will be the duty of the general government to aid them with the strength of the Union when called for. No part of this Constitution can show that this power is taken away.

Patrick Henry also said:

The 10th section of the 1st article, to which reference was made by the worthy member, militates against himself. It says, that "no state shall engage in war, unless actually invaded." If you give this clause a fair construction, what is the true meaning of it? What does this relate to? Not domestic insurrections, but war. If the country be invaded, a state may go to war, but cannot suppress insurrections. If there should happen an insurrection of slaves, the country cannot be said to be invaded. They cannot, therefore, suppress it without the interposition of Congress. The 4th section of the 4th article expressly directs that, in case of domestic violence, Congress shall protect the states on application of the legislature or executive; and the 8th section of the 1st article gives Congress power to call forth the militia to quell insurrections: there cannot, therefore, be a concurrent power. The state legislatures ought to have power to call forth the efforts of the militia, when necessary. Occasions for calling them out may be urgent, pressing, and instantaneous. The states cannot now call them, let an insurrection be ever so perilous, without an application to Congress. So long a delay may be fatal.

There are three clauses which prove, beyond the possibility of doubt, that Congress, and Congress only, can call forth the militia. The clause giving Congress power to call them out to suppress insurrections, &c.; that which restrains a state from engaging in war except when actually invaded; and that which requires Congress to protect the states against domestic violence, — render it impossible that a state can have power to intermeddle with them. Will not Congress find refuge for their actions in these clauses? With respect to the concurrent jurisdiction, it is a political monster of absurdity. We have passed that clause which gives Congress an unlimited authority over the national wealth; and here is an unbounded control over the national strength. Notwithstanding this clear, unequivocal relinquishment of the power of controlling the militia, you say the states retain it, for the very purposes given to Congress. Is it fair to say that you give the power of arming the militia, and at the same time to say you reserve it? This great national government ought not to be left in this condition. If it be, it will terminate in the destruction of our liberties.

Patrick Henry was on the side of saying that Article 1 Section 8 did not do enough to protect State control over the militia, and one of his concerns was the destruction of their liberties, such as in the case of not being able to suppress "an insurrection of slaves."

During the debates, George Mason said, "*The augmentation of slaves weakens the states; and such a trade is diabolical in itself, and disgraceful to mankind*" and "*I would not admit the Southern States into the Union unless they agree to the discontinuance of this disgraceful trade, because it would bring weakness, and not strength, to the Union.*"

While there were people like Patrick Henry saying things like, "*Among ten thousand implied powers which they may assume, they may, if we be engaged in war, liberate every one of your slaves if they please.*" There were also people like Governor Randolph saying, "*Are we not weakened by the population of those whom we hold in slavery?*" and even those who had slaves or supported its continuance called it a "bitter cup" or said they detested it. Mr. Zacharia Johnson said, "*If it were totally abolished, it would do much good.*"

While protecting their ability to keep slaves was something debated in support of the Second Amendment, one would be hard-pressed to say that the entire point of the Second Amendment was to keep people enslaved, as there was nearly universal support for State control over the militia while there was direct opposition to slavery.

The US Constitution doesn't grant rights

This is true; the US Constitution defines powers and protects certain rights, but the framers believed that we have "natural rights," as in "we have certain fundamental rights as human beings," and we have rights that result from a social compact. The fact that these rights are protected by the Constitution and not granted by the Constitution, however, has no direct relation to the Second Amendment, which doesn't grant anything. It is about limiting the government's actions.

Rights protected in the US Constitution are not absolute; they can be regulated

It is true that when the US Constitution says that individuals have a "right" to something, there is usually a situation where that can be regulated or limited. We have the Freedom of Religion, but that doesn't extend to infringing upon anyone else's rights. We have the Freedom of Speech, but that doesn't apply to Libel, Incitement, Fighting Words, Obscenity, Defamation, Commercial Speech, or in situations of Compelling Interest. We have the Freedom of the Press, but that can be limited by national security interests (classified information). We have the Freedom of Assembly, which doesn't extend to violence, vandalism, or even trespassing. Before assembling in a public space, we should check the local laws and officials to ensure the proper permissions are obtained. So even if the Second Amendment is interpreted as providing an individual right to bear arms, this doesn't mean that it cannot be regulated or limited. A few commonly accepted limitations across both theories are youth, criminal convictions, and type of arms (we do not have a personal right to nuclear weapons, for example). Ultimately though, what shall not be infringed is the people having a militia that reports to the civilian government, and that is something the Framers felt should be absolute.

The Second Amendment is so that the people can overthrow a tyrannical government

What government would legalize its own violent overthrow? Especially in its founding documents. Again, the Constitution states (Article 1 Section 8) that Congress has the power to suppress insurrection. It goes even further because it bans those who have engaged in insurrection or rebellion from public office (14th Amendment) and disavows any public debt where money was spent to support an insurrection.

Many will point to a reference by Justice Joseph Story where he says, "*The right of the citizens to keep and bear arms has justly been considered, as the palladium of the liberties of a republic; since it offers a strong moral check against the usurpation and arbitrary power of rulers*" as justification for this theory, however by "moral check" Justice Story was talking about how it is harder to order a militia to go against people they live and work with than people they don't know, he was not talking about taking arms against the government there. He does finish the sentence with "*and will generally, even if these are successful in the first instance, enable the people to resist and triumph over them,*" however this doesn't translate to legalizing taking up arms against the government, nor does it imply that the Second Amendment is about owning weapons outside the scope of the militia, as the entire passage this quote is from was about the militia. He says, "*How it is practicable to keep the people duly armed without some organization, it is difficult to see.*"

In short, the Constitution has no provision supporting the violent overthrowing of the government.

The Second Amendment, from the day it was passed, limited the type of people who could own a gun and what type of weapon you could own

This is an incorrect argument President Joe Biden put forth in a White House announcement on June 23, 2021.

The Second Amendment has never limited what type of guns or weapons people can own.

There were undoubtedly gun regulations in place when the Second Amendment was passed and after, and even after the Fourteenth Amendment introduced the incorporation doctrine. However, none of those gun regulations were dependent upon the Second Amendment.

Collective Rights mean that there are no Individual Rights

Collective rights don't always override individual rights; collective vs. individual is about scope. Therefore, the collective rights interpretation and the individual rights interpretation of the Second Amendment are talking about the scope of the amendment, not if people have individual rights or not. For example, people in a republic like the United States have a collective right to elect their leaders. Article 1 Section 2 of the Constitution says, "*The House of Representatives shall be composed of Members chosen every second Year by the People of the several States.*" The 17th Amendment also expanded this to the Senate with "*elected by the people thereof.*" We don't individually choose House Members, Senators, or anyone else in an elected position. That is not an individual right; it is a collective right. The fact that it is a collective right doesn't override our individual right to vote and participate in those elections. It depends on it. Saying the Second Amendment is about a collective right doesn't mean that no one can own a gun, nor does it talk about gun ownership outside the scope of a well-regulated militia for the security of a free State. The Second Amendment is simply about the fact that we have the right to be protected by (and apply to join) a well-regulated State Militia, it doesn't take away any individual rights or prevent private gun ownership.

Abridge *refers to individual rights,* **Infringe** *refers to encroachment on a public or sovereign right*

Abridged was used in the initial draft of the First Amendment. The House changed it to "Infringed," then the Senate changed it back to "Abridged" before confirming it. The First Amendment now says, *"The right of citizens of the United States to vote shall not be denied or abridged."* So clearly, the word usage here was important to the Framers.

Abridged is also used in the US Constitution in relation to voting rights. Our right to vote may not be *"in any way abridged, except for participation in rebellion, or other crime."* Both the right to vote and the right to free speech are universally agreed to be individual rights.

The difference here may not be as simple as "individual rights" and "collective rights." Instead, it may be in reference to whether a state can add additional limitations. A state government may not add further limitations to our right to vote or our right to free speech, which is not recognized at a federal level. However, if the Federal Government does not infringe on the State's ability to do something, then the State could add further limitations as they wish, so long as those limitations don't contradict other parts of the US Constitution - such as the Federal Government's ability to raise armies or call forth the militia.

False Quotes

Many quotes shared in Second Amendment debates cannot be verified to have been said by the person who is supposedly being quoted. The following are just a few examples.

According to The Thomas Jefferson Foundation there's no evidence that Thomas Jefferson said, "When government fears the people, there is liberty. When the people fear the government, there is tyranny." Or "The strongest reason for the people to retain the right to keep and bear arms is, as a last resort, to protect themselves against tyranny in government." Or "The beauty of the Second Amendment is that it will not be needed until they try to take it." Some of these quotes have been attributed to what he wrote in The Federalist, however Thomas Jefferson didn't contribute to the Federalist (that was the works of Alexander Hamilton, John Jay and James Madison).

The closest thing to the above quotes which Thomas Jefferson is confirmed to have said, in an 1825 letter, was:

Some are whigs, liberals, democrats, call them what you please. Others are tories, serviles, aristocrats, &c. The latter fear the people, and wish to transfer all power to the higher classes of society; the former consider the people as the safest depository of power in the last resort; they cherish them therefore, and wish to leave in them all the powers to the exercise of which they are competent.

George Washington, despite it being engraved on a plaque in Texas, did not say, "A free people ought not only be armed and disciplined, but they should have sufficient arms and ammunition to maintain a status of independence from any who might attempt to abuse them, which would include their own government."

What he actually said in the first State of the Union was:

A free people ought not only to be armed, but disciplined; to which end a uniform and well-digested plan is requisite; and their safety and interest require that they should promote such manufactories as tend to render them independent of others for essential, particularly military, supplies.

George Washington did not say that people should fight with arms and ammunition against their own government.

George Washington also did not say, "When government takes away citizens' right to bear arms it becomes citizens' duty to take away government's right to govern." This one has no known similarity to anything he said. The same goes for: "When a nation mistrusts its citizens with guns it is it sending a clear message. It no longer trusts its citizens because such a government has evil plans."

You can find out which quotes are actually attributed to George Washington and which aren't, by checking with The Washington Library from Mount Vernon.

According to the Ronald Reagan Presidential Foundation, Ronald Reagan did not say, "Under no pretext should arms and ammunition be surrendered; any attempt to disarm the workers must be frustrated, by force if necessary." That is a quote from <u>Address of the Central Committee to the Communist League</u> written by Karl Marx and Friedrich Engels in 1850 (who also authored <u>The Communist Manifesto</u>).

While Ronald Reagan didn't say the above quote, he did speak on gun control. He did say:

We will never disarm any American who seeks to protect his or her family from fear and harm,

and

you won't get gun control by disarming law abiding citizens. There's only one way to get real gun control: Disarm the thugs and the criminals, lock them up, and if you don't actually throw away the key, at least lose it for a long time.

Before believing or sharing any quote from an untrustworthy source (like an internet meme), do some research to validate if the quoted person truly said those words.

How the courts have weighed in

Gun control laws exist

In the strictest interpretation, The Individual Rights Theory would make nearly all gun control laws unconstitutional. A good gauge of whether the courts agree with The Individual Rights Theory or The Collective Rights Theory is how many states have gun control laws. Outside of the nearly three hundred Federal gun control laws, there are gun control laws in every state. In Alaska, a state that has very few gun regulations, your right to possess a firearm isn't protected until you are 16 years old, purchasing a shotgun at 18 and purchasing a handgun at 21 (the Second Amendment doesn't mention an age), and you cannot carry a gun into schools, domestic violence shelters, courts, or correctional institutions. The possession of any firearm while intoxicated is also illegal. So, the "individual" right to bear arms is being infringed upon. Texas is another state known for its love of firearms, where your right to carry a gun also isn't fully protected until you are 21 years old, and you can't carry long guns onto school campuses or any type of gun in designated "gun-free zones." While those laws seem overly lenient to many of us, they would still be abridgments to the "individual" right to bear arms. What we can gather from the Federal and State legislature is that they do not believe that the Second Amendment prevents the regulation of firearms.

The Supreme Court of the United States was established by the US Constitution, and defined by the Judiciary Act of 1789. It was first assembled in 1790 with six Justices, and it's had a variation of members from five to ten over the years. There are currently nine Justices, but many feel that they should increase this to match the number of Justices as Appellate courts that sit below it, which is currently thirteen.

At the Supreme Court level, what the courts have consistently shown is that the Second Amendment doesn't prevent strong firearm regulations.

Houston v. Moore – 1820

In 1814 the State of Pennsylvania created a law that said that officers and privates of the militia of Pennsylvania shall be liable to federal penalties if they refused to serve. The case was not primarily about the Second Amendment, it was more about the intersection of the militia clauses of Article 1 Section 8 and the Eleventh Amendment.

The Eleventh Amendment is:

The Judicial power of the United States shall not be construed to extend to any suit in law or equity, commenced or prosecuted against one of the United States by Citizens of another State, or by Citizens or Subjects of any Foreign State.

Bushrod Washington

Continental Army 1781-1783

Virginia House of Delegates 1787-1788

Supreme Court of the United States 1798-1829

The judgment of the court was delivered by Justice Washington, who started by saying that before they could begin to evaluate the case:

it will be necessary to inquire 1. what are the powers granted to the general government, by the Constitution of the United States, over the militia. and, 2. to what extent they have been assumed and exercised.

1. The Constitution declares that Congress shall have power to provide for calling forth the militia in three specified cases: for organizing, arming, and disciplining them; and for governing such part of them as may be employed in the service of the United States;

reserving to the states, respectively, the appointment of the officers, and the authority of training the militia according to the discipline prescribed by Congress. It is further provided that the President of the United States shall be commander of the militia, when called into the actual service of the United States.

2. After the Constitution went into operation, Congress proceeded by many successive acts to exercise these powers, and to provide for all the cases contemplated by the Constitution.

Thus, establishing that the case was about whether the act of the Legislature of Pennsylvania was Constitutional or not, concerning authority over the militia. He went over the matter in detail and ultimately stated that the law in question was not unconstitutional, though two of the seven Justices disagreed.

In his dissenting opinion (which is an opinion provided by the minority in disagreement with the majority), Justice Joseph Story says:

The Constitution declares that Congress shall have power "to provide for calling forth the militia to execute the laws of the Union, suppress insurrections, and repel invasions," and "to provide for organizing, arming, and disciplining the militia, and for governing such part of them as may be employed in the service of the United States, reserving to the states respectively the appointment of the officers, and the authority of training the militia according to the discipline prescribed by Congress."

It is almost too plain for argument that the power here given to Congress over the militia is of a limited nature and confined to the objects specified in these clauses, and that in all other respects and for all other purposes, the militia is subject to the control and government of the state authorities. Nor can the reservation to the states of the appointment of the officers and authority of the training the militia according to the discipline prescribed by Congress, be justly considered as weakening this conclusion. That reservation constitutes an exception merely from the power given to Congress "to provide for organizing, arming, and disciplining the militia," and is a limitation upon the authority, which would otherwise depend upon its own the appointment of officers. But the exception from a given power cannot, upon any fair reasoning, be considered as an enumeration of all the powers which belong to the states over the militia. The exception then ascertains only that Congress has not, and that the states have, the power to appoint the officers of the militia and to train them according to the discipline prescribed by Congress. Nor does it seem necessary to contend that the power "to provide for organizing, arming, and disciplining the militia" is exclusively vested in Congress. It is merely an affirmative power, and if not in its own nature incompatible with the existence of a like power in the states, it may well leave a concurrent power in the latter. But when once Congress has carried this power into effect, its laws for the organization, arming, and discipline of the militia are the supreme law of the land, and all interfering state regulations must necessarily be suspended in their operation. It would certainly seem reasonable that in the absence of all interfering provisions by Congress on the subject, the states should have authority to organize, arm, and discipline their own militia. The general authority retained by them over the militia would seem to draw after it these as necessary incidents.

He then does mention the Second Amendment; however, it is mislabeled as the Fifth Amendment:

If, therefore, the present case turned upon the question whether a state might organize, arm, and discipline its own militia in the absence of or subordinate to the regulations of Congress, I am certainly not prepared to deny the legitimacy of such an exercise of authority. It does not seem repugnant in its nature to the grant of a like paramount authority to Congress, and if not, then it is retained by the states. The Fifth Amendment to the Constitution, declaring that "a well regulated militia being necessary to the security of a free state, the right of the people to keep and bear arms shall not be infringed," may not, perhaps, be thought to have any important bearing on this point. If it have, it confirms and illustrates rather than impugns the reasoning already suggested.

What Justice Story is saying about the Second Amendment is that it confirms and illustrates the fact that states have the authority to organize, arm, and discipline their own militia without opposing the validity of Article 1 Section 8.

Like many early debates on the Second Amendment, Justice Story is talking about who controls the militia – the Federal Government or the State Government – and to what extent. In reviewing Article 1 Section 8, he says:

The remaining clause gives Congress power "to provide for calling forth the militia to execute the laws of the Union, suppress insurrections, and repel invasions." Does this clause vest in Congress an exclusive power, or leave to the states a concurrent power to enact laws for the same purposes? This is an important question, bearing directly on the case before us, and deserves serious deliberation. The plaintiff contends that the power is exclusive in Congress; the defendant that it is not.

In considering this question, it is always to be kept in view that the case is not of a new power granted to Congress where no similar power already existed in the states. On the contrary, the states, in virtue of their sovereignty, possessed general authority over their own militia, and the Constitution carved out of that a specific power in certain enumerated cases. But the grant of such a power is not necessarily exclusive unless the retaining of a concurrent power by the states be clearly repugnant to the grant. It does not strike me that there is any repugnancy in such concurrent power in the states. Why may not a state call forth its own militia in aid of the United States, to execute the laws of the Union or suppress insurrections or repel invasions? It would certainly seem fit that a state might so do where the insurrection or invasion is within its own territory and directed against its own existence or authority, and yet these are cases to which the power of Congress pointedly applies. And the execution of the laws of the Union within its territory may not be less vital to its rights and authority than the suppression of a rebellion or the repulse of an enemy. I do not say that a state may call forth, or claim under its own command, that portion of its militia which the United States has already called forth and holds employed in actual service. There would be a repugnancy in the exercise of such an authority under such circumstances. But why may it not call forth, and employ the rest of its militia in aid of the United States, for the constitutional purposes? It could not clash with the exercise of the authority confided to Congress, and yet that it must necessarily clash with it in all cases is the sole ground upon which the authority of Congress can be deemed exclusive. I am not prepared to assert that a concurrent power is not retained by the states to provide for the calling forth its own militia as auxiliary to the power of Congress in the enumerated cases. The argument of the plaintiff is that when a power is granted to Congress to legislate in specific cases for purposes growing out of the Union, the natural conclusion is that the power is designed to be exclusive. That the power is to be exercised for the good of the whole, by the will of the whole, and consistent with the interests of the whole, and that these objects can nowhere be so clearly seen or so thoroughly weighed as in Congress, where the whole nation is represented. But the argument proves too much, and pursued to its full extent, it would establish that all the powers granted to Congress are exclusive unless where concurrent authority is expressly reserved to the states.

The reason Justice Story gave as to why he disagreed with the majority is that he felt the lines between Congressional authority and State authority should be kept distinct. The Pennsylvania law was claiming authority to enforce a Federal law, while he felt that it was up to the Federal government to enforce Federal laws.

Upon the whole, I am of opinion that the courts martial intended by the act of 1795 are not state courts martial, but those of the United States, and this is the same construction which has been already put upon the same act by the Supreme Court of Pennsylvania.

What, then, is the state of the case before the Court? Congress, by a law, declared that the officers and privates of the militia who shall, when called forth by the President, fail to obey his orders shall be liable to certain penalties, to be adjudged by a court martial convened under its own authority. The Legislature of Pennsylvania inflicted the same penalties for the same disobedience, and directed these penalties to be adjudged by a state court martial called exclusively under its own authority. The offense was created by a law of the United States, and was solely against its authority and made punishable in a specific manner; the Legislature of Pennsylvania, without the assent of the United States, insisted upon being an auxiliary -- nay, as the defendant contends, a principal, if not a paramount, sovereign in its execution. This is the real state of the case, and it is said, without the slightest disrespect for the Legislature of Pennsylvania, who in passing this act was without question governed by the highest motives of patriotism, public honor, and fidelity to the Union. If it has transcended its legitimate authority, it has committed an unintentional error which it will be the first to repair and the last to vindicate. Our duty compels us, however, to compare the legislation, and not the intention, with the standard of the Constitution.

...

That there are cases in which an offense particularly aimed against the laws or authority of the United States may at the same time be directed against state authority also, and thus be within the legitimate reach of state legislation in the absence of national legislation on the same subject I pretend not to affirm or to deny. It will be sufficient to meet such a case when it shall arise. But that an offense against the constitutional authority of the United States can, after the national legislature has provided for its trial and punishment, be cognizable in a state court in virtue of a state law creating a like offense and defining its punishment, without the consent of Congress, I am very far from being ready to admit. It seems to me that such an exercise of state authority is completely open to the great objections which are presented in the case before us.

Both the majority and dissenting opinions in this case seemed to interpret the Constitution the same concerning the militia, the disagreement was about whether a State could enforce Federal laws.

Aymette v. State — 1840

Tennessee had made carrying a concealed bowie knife illegal, and it was challenged at the Supreme Court of Tennessee as being against the State Constitution. The State law of the time said *"that, if any person shall wear any bowie-knife, or Arkansas toothpick, or other knife or weapon that shall in form, shape, or size resemble a bowie-knife or Arkansas toothpick, under his clothes, or keep the same concealed about his person such person shall be guilty of a misdemeanor, and, upon conviction thereof, shall be fined in a sum not less than two hundred dollars, and shall be imprisoned in the county jail not less than three months and not more than sic months."*

The relevant part of the State Constitution at the time was "that the free white men of this State have a right to keep and bear arms for their common defence."

Judge Green, delivering the opinion of the court, references the Second Amendment directly, saying that the related portion of the State Bill of Rights (known as Article 1) should come under the same view.

In discussing the phrase "right to keep and bear arms" he says:

to keep and bear arms for what? If the history of the subject had left in doubt the object for which the rights is secured, the words that are employed must completely remove the doubt. It is declared that they may keep and bear arms for thier common defence. The word "common," here used, means, according to Webster: 1. Belonging equally to more than one, or to many indefinitely. 2. Belonging equally to the public. 3. General. 4. Universal. 5. Public. The object, then, for which the right of keeping and bearing arms is secured is the defence of the public. The free white men may keep arms to protect the public liberty, to keep in awe those who are in power, and to maintain the supremacy of the laws and the constitution. The words "bear arms," too, have reference to their military use, and were not employed to mean wearing them about the person as part of the dress. As the object for which the right to keep and bear arms is secured is of general and public nature, to be exercised by the people in a body, for their common defence, so the arms the right to keep which is secured are such as are usually employed military equipment. If the citizens have these arms in their hands, they are prepared in the best possible manner to repel any encroachments upon their rights by those in authority. They need not, for such a purpose, the use of those weapons which are usually employed in private broils, and which are efficient only in the hands of the robber and the assassin. These weapons would be useless in war. They could not be employed advantageously in common defence of the citizens. The right to keep and bear them is not, therefore, secured by the constitution.

He then calls it absurd to think that the phrase extended to any invention for inflicting death. He continues:

The right to keep and bear arms for the common defence is a great political right. It respects the citizens, on the one hand, and the rulers on the other. And, although this right must be inviolably preserved, yet it does no follow that the Legislature is prohibited altogether from passing laws regulating the manner in which these arms may be employed.

To hold that the Legislature could pass no law upon this subject by which to preserve the public peace, and protect our citizens from the terror which a wanton and unusual exhibition of arms might produce, or their lives from being endangered by desperadoes with concealed arms, would be to pervert a great political right to the worst of purposes, and to make it a social evil of infinitely greater extent to society than would result from abandoning the right itself.

...

the right to bear arms is not of that unqualified character, the citizens may bear them for the common defence; but it does not follow that they may be borne by an individual, merely to terrify the people or for purposes of private assassination.

He also touches on regulating concealed weapons, referring to a decision made by another state court:

They say there can be no difference between a law prohibiting the wearing concealed weapons and one prohibiting the wearing them openly.

We think there is a manifest distinction. In the nature of things, if they were not allowed to bear arms openly, they could not bear them in their defence of the State at all. To bear arms in defence of the State is to employ them in war, as arms are usually employed by civilized nations. The arms, consisting of swords, [161] muskets, rifles, etc., must necessarily be borne openly; so that a prohibition to bear them openly would be a denial of the right altogether. And, as in their constitution the right to bear arms in defence of themselves is coupled with the right to bear them in defence of the State, we must understand the expressions as meaning the same thing, and as relating to public, and not private, to the common, and not the individual, defence.

Then he makes the distinction between bearing arms for a military purpose and a non-military purpose very clear:

The 28th section of our bill of rights provides "that no citizen of this State shall be compelled to bear arms provided he will pay an equivalent, to be ascertained by law." Here we know that the phrase has a military sense, and no other; and we must infer that it is used in the same sense in the 26th section, which secures to the citizen the right to bear arms. A man in the pursuit of deer, elk, and buffaloes might carry his rifle every day for forty years, and yet it would never be said of him that he had borne arms; much less could it be said that a private citizen bears arms because he had a dirk or pistol concealed under his clothes, or a spear in a cane.

He concludes by saying that the state legislature was well within its rights to pass the law in question and that Aymette's constitutional rights were not infringed upon.

Dred Scott v. Sandford — 1857

Many legal scholars consider the decision from Dred Scott v. Sandford to be the worst ever rendered by the Supreme Court. In it, an enslaved man named Dred Scott and his wife sued for their freedom because they had been living in a free state. The court eventually decided that enslaved people were not citizens of the United States, so they could not expect any protection from the Federal Government or the courts. The reason the case is brought up in Second Amendment conversations is usually not to point out that enslaved people are not citizens but because the court's opinion states, *"Nor can Congress deny to the people the right to keep and bear arms, nor the right to trial by jury, nor compel anyone to be a witness against himself in a criminal proceeding."* While each of these phrases can be found in amendments, this sentence (which is the only mention of the right to bear arms in the court's decision) doesn't elaborate on what the Second Amendment means one way or another, nor does it mention the amendment by name. It is brought up in the court's opinion to make the point that the government can't take away someone's property (as in Dred Scott and his wife) just because they travel into a different territory of the United States (where slavery is illegal).

Despite ruling in favor of the slave owner, not Dred Scott, the court did provide a lengthy description of how slavery is *"hardly consistent with the respect due to these States to suppose that they regarded at that time as fellow citizens and members of the sovereignty."* The following passage mentions the ability to keep and carry arms:

More especially, it cannot be believed that the large slaveholding States regarded them as included in the word citizens, or would have consented to a Constitution which might compel them to receive them in that character from another State. For if they were so received, and entitled to the privileges and immunities of citizens, it would exempt them from the operation of the special laws and from the police regulations which they considered to be necessary for their own safety. It would give to persons of the negro race, who were recognised as citizens in any one State of the Union, the right to enter every other State whenever they pleased, singly or in companies, without pass or passport, and without obstruction, to sojourn there as long as they pleased, to go where they pleased at every hour of the day or night without molestation, unless they committed some violation of law for which a white man would be punished; and it would give them the full liberty of speech in public and in private upon all subjects upon which its own citizens might speak; to hold public meetings upon political affairs, and to keep and carry arms wherever they went.

We cannot assume that every mention of keeping, bearing, or carrying arms references the Second Amendment directly. The Second Amendment is not mentioned in that text; therefore, we should not assume that the Second Amendment is about "carrying arms wherever we go." In any case, the court did not rule that Dred Scott had a right to bear arms, it ruled that he and his wife were to remain slaves.

United States v. Cruikshank — 1876

In 1873, somewhere between 62 and 153 black militiamen were murdered by a mob of former Confederate soldiers and members of the Ku Klux Klan in Colfax, Louisiana. This was known as the Colfax massacre. Ninety-seven men involved in the massacre were indicted, and nine were charged with violating the Civil Rights Act of 1870. Three men were found guilty of sixteen charges, but a Federal Judge dismissed the convictions. When the appeal made it to the Supreme Court as United States v Cruikshank, Chief Justice Morrison R. Waite commented on a few Constitutional Amendments.

Morrison R. Waite

Ohio House of Representatives 1849-1850

Supreme Court of the United States 1874-1888

Regarding the First Amendment, he said that it only prohibited Congress from abridging the right to assemble but did not prevent State governments from doing so. He also said that the Fourteenth Amendment (which extended citizenship to freed slaves and extended Constitutional privileges or immunities to State governments) was not designed to protect individuals against the actions of other individuals. These statements run contrary to how the law is understood today.

Regarding the Second Amendment, in the majority opinion, Waite says:

The right there specified is that of "bearing arms for a lawful purpose." This is not a right granted by the Constitution. Neither is it in any manner dependent upon that instrument for its existence. The second amendment declares that it shall not be infringed, but this, as has been seen, means no more than that it shall not be infringed by Congress. This is one of the amendments that has no other effect than to restrict the powers of the national government, leaving the people to look for their protection against any violation by their fellow citizens of the rights it recognizes

The general understanding of this decision is that the right to keep and bear arms exists separately from the US Constitution, not "from" the Second Amendment.

He continues to say:

The Fourteenth Amendment prohibits a State from depriving any person of life, liberty, or property without due process of law, and from denying to any person within its jurisdiction the equal protection of the laws, but it adds nothing to the rights of one citizen as against another. It simply furnishes an additional guaranty against any encroachment by the States upon the fundamental rights which belong to every citizen as a member of society. The duty of protecting all its citizens in the enjoyment of an equality of rights was originally assumed by the States, and it still remains there. The only obligation resting upon the United States is to see that the States do not deny the right. This the Amendment guarantees, but no more. The power of the National Government is limited to the enforcement of this guaranty.

The States initially assumed the duty of protecting all its citizens in the enjoyment of an equality of rights and still remains there and the Second Amendment does not create a "right of bearing arms for a lawful purpose." Even if we do assume that "right of bearing arms for a lawful purpose" is what the Second Amendment, that lawful purpose is described in Article 1 Section 8.

Presser v. Illinois — 1886

Herman Presser was part of a citizen militia group formed to counter the armed forces of private companies in Chicago. In 1879 he marched at the head of about four hundred members of that militia group, armed with rifles while Presser himself had a cavalry sword, in the streets of Chicago. He was indicted for this because he "*did unlawfully belong to, and did parade and drill in the city of Chicago with an unauthorized body of men with arms, who had associated themselves together as a military company and organization, without having a license from the Governor, and not being a part of, or belonging to, 'the regular organized volunteer militia' of the State of Illinois, or the troops of the United States.*" Presser claimed that his rights were violated under the Second Amendment.

William Burnham Woods

US Army 1862-1866

US Circuit Court for the Fifth Circuit 1869-1880

Supreme Court of the United States 1881-1887

When the case made it to the Supreme Court, Justice Woods delivered the opinion of the court. They said that the Second Amendment existed only to limit the Federal Government and not the State Government, similar to United States v Cruikshank (the court's opinion on this would later change). They stated, "*Unless restrained by their own constitutions, state legislatures may enact statutes to control and regulate all organizations, drilling, and parading of military bodies and associations except those which are authorized by the militia laws of the United States.*"

They clarified that the Second Amendment did prevent the national and state governments from passing laws that would be so strict as to deprive the government of the well-regulated militia:

The provision in the Second Amendment to the Constitution, that "The right of the people to keep and bear arms shall not be infringed" is a limitation only on the power of Congress and the national government, and not of the states. But in view of the fact that all citizens capable of bearing arms constitute the reserved military force of the national government as well as in view of its general powers, the states cannot prohibit the people from keeping and bearing arms so as to deprive the United States of their rightful resource for maintaining the public security.

Since Presser was charged under Military Code, they reviewed the constitutionality of those sections:

We are next to inquire whether the 5th and 6th sections of Article XI of the Military Code are in violation of the other provisions of the Constitution of the United States relied on by the plaintiff in error. The first of these is the Second Amendment, which declares: "A well regulated militia being necessary to the security of a free state, the right of the people to keep and bear arms shall not be infringed."

We think it clear that the sections under consideration, which only forbid bodies of men to associate together as military organizations, or to drill or parade with arms in cities and towns unless authorized by law, do not infringe the right of the people to keep and bear arms. But a conclusive answer to the contention that this amendment prohibits the legislation in question lies in the fact that the amendment is a limitation only upon the power of Congress and the national government, and not upon that of the state.

They then said:

It is undoubtedly true that all citizens capable of bearing arms constitute the reserved military force or reserve militia of the United

States as well as of the states, and, in view of this prerogative of the general government, as well as of its general powers, the states cannot, even laying the constitutional provision in question out of view, prohibit the people from keeping and bearing arms so as to deprive the United States of their rightful resource for maintaining the public security, and disable the people from performing their duty to the general government. But as already stated, we think it clear that the sections under consideration do not have this effect.

Thus, they were saying that the Second Amendment is about ensuring public security through a duty to the general government.

The court made sure to point out that Presser was not a member of the Illinois militia:

The plaintiff in error was not a member of the organized volunteer militia of the State of Illinois, nor did he belong to the troops of the United States or to any organization under the militia law of the United States. On the contrary, the fact that he did not belong to the organized militia or the troops of the United States was an ingredient in the offense for which he was convicted and sentenced. The question is therefore had he a right as a citizen of the United States, in disobedience of the state law, to associate with others as a military company and to drill and parade with arms in the towns and cities of the state? If the plaintiff in error has any such privilege, he must be able to point to the provision of the Constitution or statutes of the United States by which it is conferred. For, as was said by this Court in United States v. Cruikshank, 92 U. S. 542, 92 U. S. 551, 92 U. S. 560, the government of the United States, although it is "within the scope of its powers supreme and above the states, . . . can neither grant nor secure to its citizens any right or privilege not expressly or by implication placed under its jurisdiction. . . . All that cannot be so granted or so secured are left to the exclusive protection of the state."

We have not been referred to any statute of the United States which confers upon the plaintiff in error the privilege which he asserts.

…

Military organization and military drill and parade under arms are subjects especially under the control of the government of every country. They cannot be claimed as a right independent of law.

Presser lost his case. The court affirmed that States can regulate militias. The decision also says States may not disarm the people to such an extent that there is no remaining armed militia force for the federal government to call upon, as per Article 1 Section 8, which gives the Federal Government the power to call forth the armed militia.

Logan v. United States — 1892

In 1891 a case that was the end of a long and winding adventure made it to the Supreme Court. The real-life story inspired the movie The Sons of Katie Elder. What reached the Supreme Court was whether US citizens in custody have a right to be protected by the United States against lawless violence. The issue arose because while the defendants were in custody in Weatherford, Texas, the deputies who were supposed to guard them abandoned their post, and a mob attacked the jail, trying to get at them. The men had defended themselves and successfully fended off the mob.

The Supreme Court ruled that "*A citizen of the United States, in the custody of a United States Marshall under a lawful commitment to answer for an offense against the United States, has the right to be protected by the United States against lawless violence; this right is a right secured to him by the Constitution and laws of the United States, and a conspiracy to injure or oppress him in its free exercise or enjoyment is punishable under section 5508 of the Revised Statutes.*"

The decision mentioned the previous United States v. Cruikshank case but was not directly based on the Second Amendment.

It was held that the second amendment of the Constitution, declaring that "the right of the people to keep and bear arms shall not be infringed," was equally limited in its scope.

Robertson v. Baldwin — 1897

In 1895 the District Court for the Northern District of California dismissed a writ of habeas corpus (legal order to determine if a person is lawfully imprisoned) for a group of seamen detained for abandoning their contract to serve on the vessel Arago. The case was largely based on the 13th Amendment, which reads:

Neither slavery nor involuntary servitude, except as a punishment for crime whereof the party shall have been duly convicted, shall exist within the United States, or any place subject to their jurisdiction.

Thus, if detaining sailors for desertion is or isn't constitutional. In the opinion by the Supreme Court, the scope of the Second Amendment was mentioned:

The law is perfectly well settled that the first ten amendments to the Constitution, commonly known as the "Bill of Rights," were not intended to lay down any novel principles of government, but simply to embody certain guaranties and immunities which we had inherited from our English ancestors, and which had, from time immemorial, been subject to certain well recognized exceptions arising from the necessities of the case. In incorporating these principles into the fundamental law, there was no intention of disregarding the exceptions, which continued to be recognized as if they had been formally expressed. Thus, the freedom of speech and of the press (Art. I) does not permit the publication of libels, blasphemous or indecent articles, or other publications injurious to public morals or private reputation; the right of the people to keep and bear arms (Art. II) is not infringed by laws prohibiting the carrying of concealed weapons; the provision that no person shall be twice put in jeopardy (Art. V) does not prevent a second trial if upon the first trial the jury failed to agree or if the verdict was set aside upon the defendant's motion...

This understanding that concealed weapon restrictions does

not contradict the Second Amendment opposes modern "Constitutional Carry" laws, which imply that the opposite is true.

Ultimately the Supreme Court ruled that it is Constitutional for a seaman to be detained for desertion, it does not qualify as slavery if they signed a contract saying that they will stay with a vessel for a certain amount of time.

The decision was not unanimous, Justice Harlan wrote a dissenting opinion where he stated:

As to involuntary servitude, it may exist in the United States, but it can only exist lawfully as a punishment for crime of which the party shall have been duly convicted. Such is the plain reading of the Constitution. A condition of enforced service, even for a limited period, in the private business of another is a condition of involuntary servitude.

He continued:

I am unable to understand how the necessity for the protection of seamen against those who take advantage of them can be made the basis of legislation compelling them, against their will and by force, to render personal service for others engaged in private business. Their supposed helpless condition is thus made the excuse for imposing upon them burdens that could not be imposed upon other classes without depriving them of rights that inhere in personal freedom. The Constitution furnishes no authority for any such distinction between classes of persons in this country. If, prior to the adoption of the Thirteenth Amendment, the arrest of a seaman, and his forcible return, under any circumstances, to the vessel on which he had engaged to serve could have been authorized by an act of Congress, such deprivation of the liberty of a freeman cannot be justified under the Constitution as it now is. To give any other construction to the Constitution is to say that it is not made for all, and that all men in this land are not free and equal before the law, but that one class may be so far subjected to involuntary servitude as to be compelled by force to render personal services in a purely private business with which the public has no concern whatever.

He concludes with:

In my judgment, the holding of any person in custody, whether in jail or by an officer of the law, against his will for the purpose of compelling him to render personal service to another in a private business places the person so held in custody in a condition of involuntary servitude forbidden by the Constitution of the United States; consequently, that the statute as it now is, and under which the appellants were arrested at Astoria and placed against their will on the barkentine Arago, is null and void, and their refusal to work on such vessel after being forcibly returned to it could not be made a public offense, authorizing their subsequent arrest at San Francisco.

The current law (over Merchant Mariners) states that "*For desertion, the seaman forfeits any part of the money or property the seaman leaves on board and any part of earned wages.*" – and only allows for the confinement of seaman for not following orders while the vessel is still at sea, not imprisonment. However, if the desertion causes additional expenses the seaman may be required to provide compensation or pay a penalty of twice the expenses caused.

United States v. Schwimmer — 1929

In 1921 a Hungarian citizen named Rosika Schwimmer fled to the US. She worked with Henry Ford to try and end World War I. Then in 1926, she applied for naturalization. While applying for US citizenship, she was asked on a form if she was *"willing to take up arms in defense of this country,"* and she filled in, *"I would not take up arms personally."* As a supporter of pacifist causes, it was a line she had no desire to cross. Her application was denied because of that answer.

When the case reached the Supreme Court, they ruled that immigrants could be denied citizenship for such an answer. In the majority ruling, they said, *"The influence of conscientious objectors against the use of military force in defense of the principles of our government is apt to be more detrimental than their mere refusal to bear arms. The fact that, by reason of sex, age, or other cause, they may be unfit to serve does not lessen their purpose or power to influence others."* Their concern was in the integrity and capability of US military forces, not necessarily that she was unwilling to take up arms.

Oliver Wendell Holmes Jr.

Massachusetts Supreme Judicial Court
1882-1902

Supreme Court of the United States
1902-1932

The case has no direct relation to the Second Amendment; however, the dissent by Justice Holmes Jr. includes a meaningful perspective on the First Amendment. After stating that he did not agree with her pacifist views, he says, *"if there is any principle of the Constitution that more imperatively calls for attachment than any other, it is the principle of free thought — not free thought for those who agree with us, but freedom for the thought that we hate. I think that we should adhere to that principle with regard to admission into, as well as to life within, this country."* Justice Brandeis concurred with this opinion.

Hamilton v. Regents of the University of California — 1934

In 1931, California started requiring state college students to be involved in some form of military training. Some of the students and their parents, who had ties to the Methodist Episcopal Church and the Epworth League, disagreed with the requirement that students of the University of California had to receive instruction and discipline in military tactics. It was a case based on the requirement of military training infringing upon students' right to religious freedom protected by the First Amendment.

Unlike United States v. Schwimmer, the Supreme Court did reference the Second Amendment when they said, "*Undoubtedly every state has authority to train its able-bodied male citizens of suitable age appropriately to develop fitness, should any such duty be laid upon them, to serve in the United States Army or in state militia (always liable to be called forth by federal authority to execute the laws of the Union, suppress insurrection, or repel invasion, Constitution, Art. I, § 8, cls. 12, 15 and 16.Selective Draft Law Cases,* **245 U. S. 366, 245 U. S. 380–383**;*State v. Industrial Comm'n,186 Wis. 1, 202 N.W.191) or as members of local constabulary forces or as officers needed effectively to police the state.*" They also said, "*So long as its action is within retained powers and not inconsistent with any exertion of the authority of the national government and transgresses no right safeguarded to the citizen by the Federal Constitution, the state is the sole judge of the means to be employed and the amount of training to be exacted for the effective accomplishment of these ends. Second Amendment;*Houston v. Moore, 5 Wheat. 1,*18 U. S. 16–17*;Dunne v. People, 94 Ill. 120, 129; 1 Kent's Commentaries, 265, 389. Cf. Presser v. Illinois, 116 U. S. 252.*"

The concern here focuses on the State's right to a militia and goes further by saying that "the state is the sole judge of the means to be employed and the amount of training to be exacted for the effective accomplishment of these ends."

Benjamin N. Cardozo

Supreme Court of New York 1914-1917

New York Court of Appeals 1917-1932

Supreme Court of the United States 1932-1938

Ultimately, the Supreme Court decided that the military training requirement did not go against the Freedom of Religion. Justice Cardozo said, "*This may be condemned by some as unwise or illiberal or unfair,*". He continued with, "*Neither directly nor indirectly is government establishing a state religion when it insists upon such training. Instruction in military science, unaccompanied here by any pledge of military service, is not an interference by the state with the free exercise of religion when the liberties of the Constitution are read in the light of a century and a half of history during days of peace and war.*"

United States v. Miller — 1939

Jack Miller and Frank Layton were accused of going against the National Firearms Act of 1934 when they tried transporting a sawed-off shotgun in interstate commerce. They claimed the charge was bogus as it violated their Second Amendment right to keep and bear arms. The majority ruling stated that the charge was "*Not violative of the Second Amendment of the Federal Constitution.*"

James Clark McReynolds

US Attorney General 1913-1914

Supreme Court of the United States 1914-1941

Justice McReynolds wrote the court's unanimous decision. He reviewed the historical context of what constituted a militia:

The Militia which the States were expected to maintain and train is set in contrast with Troops which they were forbidden to keep without the consent of Congress. The sentiment of the time strongly disfavored standing armies; the common view was that adequate defense of country and laws could be secured through the Militia — civilians primarily, soldiers on occasion.

The signification attributed to the term Militia appears from the debates in the Convention, the history and legislation of Colonies and States, and the writings of approved commentators. These show plainly enough that the Militia comprised all males physically capable of acting in concert for the common defense. "A body of citizens enrolled for military discipline." And further, that ordinarily, when called for service these men were expected to appear bearing arms supplied by themselves and of the kind in common use at the time.

Justice McReynolds wasn't saying that the Second Amendment applied to every instance of the term Militia; he provided context for what the term militia meant to the Framers and historical reference for where their arms came from "supplied by themselves." While militia members may have been expected to supply their own arms, the Second Amendment certainly doesn't mandate it. After that quote, he continued to discuss militias and how all states have provisions where they regulate and organize their militias.

He reflected:

Most if not all of the States have adopted provisions touching the right to keep and bear arms. Differences in the language employed in these have naturally led to somewhat variant conclusions concerning the scope of the right guaranteed. But none of them seems to afford any material support for the challenged ruling of the court below.

The "ruling of the court below" was the district court decision that Miller's Second Amendment Rights had not been infringed upon.

The court focused on the "being necessary to the security of a free State" part of the Second Amendment, with Justice McReynolds stating:

In the absence of any evidence tending to show that possession or use of a 'shotgun having a barrel of less than eighteen inches in length' at this time has some reasonable relationship to the preservation or efficiency of a well regulated militia, we cannot say that the Second Amendment guarantees the right to keep and bear such an instrument. Certainly it is not within judicial notice that this weapon is any part of the ordinary military equipment, or that its use could contribute to the common defense.

Directly defining the purpose and scope of the Second Amendment, Justice McReynolds said:

The Constitution, as originally adopted, granted to the Congress power —

"To provide for calling forth the Militia to execute the Laws of the Union, suppress Insurrections and repel Invasions; To provide for organizing, arming, and disciplining, the Militia, and for governing such Part of them as may be employed in the Service of the United States, reserving to the States respectively, the Appointment of the Officers, and the Authority of training the Militia according to the discipline prescribed by Congress."

With obvious purpose to assure the continuation and render possible the effectiveness of such forces, the declaration and guarantee of the Second Amendment were made. It must be interpreted and applied with that end in view.

Overall, the court's statement perfectly supports and explains the Framer's original intent with the Second Amendment, however, because they offered the reasoning that the type of gun was related to this not being a violation of the Second Amendment, this opened the door to some who believe that it does protect the individual right to own types of weapons more suited to contributing to the common defense.

Burton v. Sills — 1969

In the 1960s, when New Jersey established a new Gun Control Law, a few people with sportsmen's clubs, two gun dealers, and a corporation organized to promote the sports of shooting and marksmanship sued the state, claiming that New Jersey could not regulate guns due to the Second Amendment.

The Supreme Court dismissed the case for "*want of a substantial federal question.*" In other words, the Second Amendment does not invalidate a State Legislature from regulating arms within their state.

The Supreme Court of the United States has refused to hear countless cases where various state gun laws were being challenged based on the Second Amendment, including ten on June 15th, 2020. Burton v. Sills is only one example of many.

Laird v. Tatum — 1972

The executive secretary of the Central Committee for Conscientious Objectors sued the Secretary of Defense after finding out about the US military gathering intelligence on civilians and civil organizations in the US. The claim wasn't that it infringed upon Second Amendment Rights, but First Amendment rights and the ability to express political objections.

The Supreme Court dismissed the case saying, "*the mere existence of this data-gathering system does not constitute a justiciable controversy on the basis of the record in this case, disclosing as it does no showing of objective harm or threat of specific future harm.*"

In the majority opinion, written by Chief Justice Warren Burger, the Second Amendment is mentioned: "*They were reluctant to ratify the Constitution without further assurances, and thus we find in the Bill of Rights Amendments 2 and 3, specifically authorizing a decentralized militia, guaranteeing the right of the people to keep and bear arms, and prohibiting the quartering of troops in any house in time of peace without the consent of the owner.*"

This statement of "authorizing a decentralized militia" speaks to the fact that the purpose of the Second Amendment was an authorized militia, decentralized from the federal government (authorized by the State government, not the National government).

Moore v. East Cleveland — 1977

In 1966 East Cleveland, Ohio, passed a rule saying that those living in a housing unit were limited to *"members of a single family."* This became an issue when a family was told that a grandson living with his grandparents was an *"illegal occupant"* because he didn't fit within the city's definition of a *"single family."*

When it reached the Supreme Court, they ruled that zoning ordinances cannot restrict members of a traditional family from living together.

The Second Amendment is not mentioned in the ruling; however, "the right to keep and bear arms" is mentioned in the discussion of rights.

[T]he full scope of the liberty guaranteed by the Due Process Clause cannot be found in or limited by the precise terms of the specific guarantees elsewhere provided in the Constitution. This 'liberty' is not a series of isolated points pricked out in terms of the taking of property; the freedom of speech, press, and religion; the right to keep and bear arms; the freedom from unreasonable searches and seizures; and so on. It is a rational continuum which, broadly speaking, includes a freedom from all substantial arbitrary impositions and purposeless restraints, . . . and which also recognizes what a reasonable and sensitive judgment must, that certain interests require particularly careful scrutiny of the state needs asserted to justify their abridgment.

This case not being about gun ownership but about families being able to live together, plus the abstract way that the right to bear arms is listed means the case ruling doesn't directly discuss the meaning of the Second Amendment.

Lewis v. United States — 1980

The plaintiff, in this case, had a prior conviction in Florida. He was later arrested in Virginia and charged with the unlawful possession of firearms in violation of 18 U.S.C. App. § 1202(a)(1), which reads:

SEC. 1201. The Congress hereby finds and declares that the receipt, possession, or transportation of a firearm by felons, veterans who are other than honorably discharged, mental aliens who are illegally in the country, and former citizens who have renounced their citizenship, constitutes —
(1) burden on commerce or threat affecting the free flow of commerce
(2) a threat to the safety of the President of the United States and Vice President of the United States,
(3) an impediment or a threat to the exercise of free speech and the free exercise of religion guaranteed by the first amendment to the Constitution of the United States, and
(4) a threat to the continued and effective operation of the Government of the United States and of the government of each State guaranteed by article IV of the Constitution.

SEC. 1202. (a) Any person who —
(1) has convicted by a court of the United States or of a State or any political subdivision thereof of a felony, or
(2) has discharged from the Armed Forces under other than honorable conditions, or
(3) has been adjudged by a court of the United States or of a State or any political subdivision thereof of mentally incompetent, or
(4) waving a citizen of the United States has his citizenship, or
(5) being an alien is illegally or unlawfully in the United States,
and who receives, possesses, or transports in commerce or affecting commerce, after the date of enactment of this Act, any firearm shall be fined not more than $10,000 or imprisoned for not more than two years, or both.

This case seems to some to directly challenge federal gun

control laws. However, the claim wasn't about whether the abovementioned gun control was legal. This case was actually about a much more focused scenario: if someone who didn't have a fair trial previously could be convicted of another crime that depended on their felony status.

In the previous Florida conviction, the plaintiff claimed that he had been denied counsel, a guaranteed right under the Sixth and Fourteenth Amendments.

The Supreme Court held that if a defendant's rights under the Sixth and Fourteenth Amendments are not respected for a trial, that could be a reason to challenge the decisions from that trial — it could not be used as the reason to challenge later charges, such as the federal gun control law the plaintiff, in this case, was convicted of violating.

The opinion of the court does mention past decisions related to the Second Amendment, including the quote from United States v Miller:

the Second Amendment guarantees no right to keep and bear a firearm that does not have "some reasonable relationship to the preservation or efficiency of a well regulated militia"

Overall, this case doesn't directly impact the meaning of the Second Amendment. It was based primarily on the right to proper counsel, but it does reference the purpose of the Second Amendment from United States v Miller.

The related laws, §§1201 to 1203, were repealed in 1986 as part of the Firearms Owners' Protection Act (FOPA) which revised and added firearms restrictions, such as prohibiting the transfer or possession of machine guns.

Hickman v. Block — 1996

Douglas Ray Hickman, an owner and operator of a security company and federally licensed arms dealer, tried to expand his business to include "executive protection" and thus applied for concealed firearms permits. His applications were denied, so he filed suit to claim that his Second Amendment rights were violated, among other things. It reached the US Court of Appeals for the Ninth Circuit for the Eastern District of California.

In the majority opinion written by Circuit Judge Cynthia Holcomb Hall, it was ruled that Hickman's Second Right Amendments were not violated because he failed to show how he was injured regarding the state's right to keep an armed militia.

In response to Hickman's argument that the Second Amendment is about an individual right to own arms, she says *"We follow our sister circuits in holding that the Second Amendment is a right held by the states, and does not protect the possession of a weapon by a private citizen."* She also references United States v. Miller:

This case turns on the first constitutional standing element: whether Hickman has shown injury to an interest protected by the Second Amendment. We note at the outset that no individual has ever succeeded in demonstrating such injury in federal court. The seminal authority in this area continues to be United States v. Miller, 307 U.S. 174 (1939), in which the Supreme Court upheld a conviction under the National Firearms Act, 26 U.S.C. § 1132 (1934), for transporting a sawed-off shotgun in interstate commerce. The Court rejected the appellant's hypothesis that the Second Amendment protected his possession of that weapon. Consulting the text and history of the amendment, the Court found that the right to keep and bear arms is meant solely to protect the right of the states to keep and maintain armed militia.

...

The Court's understanding follows a plain reading of the Amendment's text. The Amendment's second clause declares that the goal is to preserve the security of "a free state;" its first clause establishes the premise that a well-regulated militia are necessary to this end. Thus it is only in furtherance of state security that "the right of the people to keep and bear arms" is finally proclaimed.

On the point of standing, she says *"Because the Second Amendment guarantees the right of the states to maintain armed militia, the states alone stand in the position to show legal injury when this right is infringed."*

Hickman argued that individuals have the right to complain about the manner in which a state arms its citizens, but Judge Hall disagreed. *"The Second Amendment creates a right, not a duty. It does not oblige the states to keep an armed militia, or to arm their citizens generally, although some states do preserve, nominally at least, a broad individual right to bear arms as a foundation for their state militia."*

One of her primary points was that this wasn't a matter for the courts at all, as military matters on things such as how militias are run are largely up to the military. *"Hickman's claim amounts to a "generalized grievance" regarding the organization and training of a state militia. See Lujan, 112 S.Ct. at 2144. We do not involve ourselves in such matters. As the Supreme Court has observed, "decisions as to the composition, training, equipping, and control of a military force are essentially professional military judgments," and as such are nonjusticiable."*

Printz v. United States — 1997

Unlike Lewis v. United States, which only seemed to directly challenge federal gun control laws, Printz v. United States actually did. The Gun Control Act of 1968 prohibited firearms to individuals in certain categories, primarily based on a previous conviction of crimes, outstanding federal warrants, or certain diagnosed mental health issues. In 1993 The Brady Act required the Department of Justice to establish a federal background check system to prevent gun sales to those already prohibited from owning firearms.

The case here was based on the constitutionality of Congress requiring state officers to execute federal laws as opposed to state laws. The part of the US Constitution in question was NOT the Second Amendment, but the Tenth Amendment.

The powers not delegated to the United States by the Constitution, nor prohibited by it to the States, are reserved to the States respectively, or to the people."

Not only had the lower courts been divided on the constitutionality question raised in this case, with some deciding in favor of the law being Constitutional and others deciding that certain provisions were not Constitutional when the Supreme Court decision was divided as well.

The majority opinion was that certain parts of the Brady Act were unconstitutional, specifically the areas that required sheriffs to perform background checks. They stated that a state could put that requirement in place, but not the Federal Government.

Four of the Nine Justices dissented, giving various examples of evidence that Congress should have the power to ensure that laws constitutionally issued are enforced.

Muscarello v. United States — 1998

In this case, Frank J. Muscarello had been arrested for selling marijuana. Because he had a gun in his glove compartment, it was deemed a violation of 18 U. S. C. § 924(c)(I) — which has a mandatory 5-year prison term. Before reaching the Supreme Court, Muscarello's case was consolidated with another, where people were arrested for trying to steal drugs, and firearms were found in the trunk of their vehicle. The question put before the Supreme Court was if the phrase *"uses or carries a firearm"* extends to that firearm being not just on the person but in their vehicle in relation to drug trafficking charges.

The Supreme Court decided that yes; if a gun is in the vehicle of someone, that counts as "carrying" a firearm under the law.

This ruling does not contradict the ability of the federal government to enact gun control laws, such as 18 U. S. C. § 924(c)(I). The dissenting opinion is no different, as the disagreement was on what counts as "carrying" a firearm, not if the Federal Government could enact or enforce gun control laws.

United States v. Emerson — 2001

In 1998, a Texan named Timothy Joe Emerson's wife filed for divorce and a restraining order. During the hearing, she testified that he had threatened to kill someone. 18 U.S.C. § 922(g) (8) says that it is unlawful to own a firearm while such a restraining order is in place. Emerson's position was that the law in question was unconstitutional due to the Second, Fifth, and Tenth Amendments. The case made it to the US Court of Appeals for the Fifth Circuit, which upheld that 18 U.S.C. § 922(g) (8) was constitutional and Emerson's Constitutional rights were not infringed upon. However, it was the first federal appellate court decision to appear to side with the Individual Rights interpretation of the Second Amendment, though it had nothing to do with why the case was decided the way it was.

Judge Garwood separated his opinion into several sections, in his Section V he focused on the interpretation of the Second Amendment. He reviewed not two but three interpretations of the Second Amendment.

1. States' Rights – The Second Amendment does not apply to individuals; rather, it merely recognizes the right of a state to arm its militia.
2. Sophisticated Collective Rights – The Second Amendment recognizes some limited species of individual right. However, this right to bear arms can only be exercised by members of a function, organized state militia who bears the arms while and as a part of actively participating in the organized militia's activities. The "individual" right to keep arms only applies to members of such a militia, and then only if the federal and state governments fail to provide the firearms necessary for such militia service. At present, virtually the only such organized and actively functioning militia is the National Guard, and this has been the case for many years. Currently, the federal

government provides the necessary implements of warfare, including firearms, to the National Guard, and this likewise has long been the case.
3. Individual Rights – The Second Amendment simply recognized the right of individuals to keep and bear arms.

Note that none of those three is the interpretation that had most commonly been used by the courts, that the Second Amendment protects the right of the people to assemble a well-regulated state militia.

In reviewing stare decisis (a legal term which means "to stand by things decided", i.e. the courts typically try to be consistent in their rulings), Judge Garwood said that the government understood the United States v. Miller decision as supporting the collective rights or sophisticated collective model and rejecting the individual rights model, but he disagreed.

According to Judge Garwood, the Supreme Court in United States v. Miller the most important quote was:

In the absence of any evidence tending to show that possession or use of a 'shotgun having a barrel of less than eighteen inches in length' at this time has some reasonable relationship to the preservation or efficiency of a well regulated militia, we cannot say that the Second Amendment guarantees the right to keep and bear such an instrument. Certainly it is not within judicial notice that this weapon is any part of the ordinary military equipment or that its use could contribute to the common defense. Aymette v. State of Tennessee, 2 Humph., Tenn. 154, 158.

That section is recognized by many as pointing out that Miller and his companions were not part of the well-regulated militia (or at least were not acting on behalf of such a militia, since the guns in question were not issued to them by that militia), however, Judge Garwood didn't see it that way. He said:

Nowhere in the Court's Miller opinion is there any reference to the fact that the indictment does not remotely suggest that either of the two defendants was ever a member of any organized, active militia, such as the National Guard, much less that either was engaged (or about to be engaged) in any actual military service or training of such a militia unit when transporting the sawed-off shotgun from Oklahoma into Arkansas. Had the lack of such membership or engagement been a ground of the decision in Miller, the Court's opinion would obviously have made mention of it. But it did not.

He then points out that the Supreme Court concluded with:

The Constitution, as originally adopted, granted to the Congress power-

"To provide for calling forth the Militia to execute the Laws of the Union, suppress Insurrections and repel Invasions; To provide for organizing, arming, and disciplining, the Militia, and for governing such Part of them as may be employed in the Service of the United States, reserving to the States respectively, the Appointment of the Officers, and the Authority of training the Militia according to the discipline prescribed by Congress."

With obvious purpose to assure the continuation and render possible the effectiveness of such forces, the declaration and guarantee of the Second Amendment were made. It must be interpreted and applied with that end in view.

In United States v. Miller, the court provided some history as to what constituted a militia in the early U.S., and Judge Garwood highlighted this part:

The signification attributed to the term Militia appears from the debates in the Convention, the history and legislation of Colonies and States, and the writings of approved commentators. These show plainly enough that the Militia comprised all males physically capable of acting in concert for the common defense. "A body of citizens enrolled for military discipline." And further, that ordinarily, when called for service these men were expected to appear bearing arms supplied by themselves and of the kind in common use at the time.

While this could be taken as just historical context, Judge Garwood thought there was more to it:

These passages from Miller suggest that the militia, the assurance of whose continuation and the rendering possible of whose effectiveness Miller says were purposes of the Second Amendment, referred to the generality of the civilian male inhabitants throughout their lives from teenage years until old age and to their personally keeping their own arms, and not merely to individuals during the time (if any) they might be actively engaged in actual military service or only to those who were members of special or select units.

We conclude that Miller does not support the government's collective rights or sophisticated collective rights approach to the Second Amendment.

He did admit that the Miller decision doesn't support the Individual Rights interpretation, thus opening the door for him to introduce his own interpretation.

However, we do not proceed on the assumption that Miller actually accepted an individual rights, as opposed to a collective or sophisticated collective rights, interpretation of the Second Amendment. Thus, Miller itself does not resolve that issue. We turn, therefore, to an analysis of history and wording of the Second Amendment for guidance. In undertaking this analysis, we are mindful that almost all of our sister circuits have rejected any individual rights view of the Second Amendment. However, it respectfully appears to us that all or almost all of these opinions seem to have done so either on the erroneous assumption that Miller resolved that issue or without sufficient articulated examination of the history and text of the Second Amendment.

He proceeds down a path we see later in D.C. v. Heller, where he goes over specific words and phrases in the Second Amendment. He says "people" means "people" not government, thus the states' rights model is incorrect. Remember that James Madison said:

The federal and State governments are in fact but different agents and trustees of the people, constituted with different powers, and designed for different purposes.

Judge Garwood said that proponents of the states' rights and sophisticated collective rights models argue that the phrase "bear arms" only applies to a member of the militia carrying weapons during actual militia service, but champions of the individual rights model say that "bear arms" refers to carrying any weapons, whether by a soldier or civilian. He says there's no real question about the first, it's only the second that's an issue.

He said "keep... Arms" is an individual rather than a collective right, and not limited to National Guard members. He dismissed the second half of the Second Amendment supporting the states' rights model or the sophisticated collective rights model, then dismissed the first half of the sentence since it contradicts what he sees as the plain meaning of the second half.

He then went into the history of how the Second Amendment came about, describing the two main factions at the time as the Federalists who were for a strong federal government, and the Anti-Federalists who wanted safeguards in place to protect the people and the states from the federal government having too much power but went well beyond the discussions that the Founders had of the Second Amendment. He reviewed similar state laws that expanded into a right to self-defense, failed amendment proposals, and correspondences people had about arms in various contexts. He concluded that the Anti-Federalists supported the idea that gun ownership should be a protected right in the Bill of Rights.

He eventually claimed victory over the first two models he introduced earlier:

We have found no historical evidence that the Second Amendment was intended to convey militia power to the states, limit the federal government's power to maintain a standing army, or applies only to members of a select militia while on active duty. All of the evidence indicates that the Second Amendment, like other parts of the Bill of Rights, applies to and protects individual Americans.

We find that the history of the Second Amendment reinforces the plain meaning of its text, namely that it protects individual Americans in their right to keep and bear arms whether or not they are a member of a select militia or performing active military service or training.

…

We reject the collective rights and sophisticated collective rights models for interpreting the Second Amendment. We hold, consistent with Miller, that it protects the right of individuals

Judge Garwood continued:

including those not then actually a member of any militia or engaged in active military service or training, to privately possess and bear their own firearms, such as the pistol involved here, that are suitable as personal, individual weapons and are not of the general kind or type excluded by Miller.

Here Judge Garwood is contradicting what he said earlier, that the Miller decision did not support the Individual Rights model. His view of the Second Amendment being about the private possession of arms is not without limits, as he says that *"it is clear that felons, infants and those of unsound mind may be prohibited from possessing firearms."*

He concluded the opinion with:

We agree with the district court that the Second Amendment protects the right of individuals to privately keep and bear their own firearms that are suitable as individual, personal weapons and are not of the general kind or type excluded by Miller, regardless of whether the particular individual is then actually a member of a militia. However, for the reasons stated, we also conclude that the predicate order in question here is sufficient, albeit likely minimally so, to support the deprivation, while it remains in effect, of the defendant's Second Amendment rights. Accordingly, we reverse the district court's dismissal of the indictment on Second Amendment grounds.

We remand the cause for further proceedings not inconsistent herewith.

In his concurring opinion, Judge Robert M. Parker declined to agree to Judge Garwood's Section V, which was about the right to keep and bear arms under the Second Amendment being an individual right. He says it is dicta (a comment, suggestion, or observation that's not required) and thus not binding. He said:

The determination whether the rights bestowed by the Second Amendment are collective or individual is entirely unnecessary to resolve this case and has no bearing on the judgment we dictate by this opinion.

...

No doubt the special interests and academics on both sides of this debate will take great interest in the fact that at long last some court has determined (albeit in dicta) that the Second Amendment bestows an individual right. The real issue, however, is the fact that whatever the nature or parameters of the Second Amendment right, be it collective or individual, it is a right subject to reasonable regulation. The debate, therefore, over the nature of the right is misplaced. In the final analysis, whether the right to keep and bear arms is collective or individual is of no legal consequence. It is, as duly noted by the majority opinion, a right subject to reasonable regulation. If determining that Emerson had an individual Second Amendment right that could have been successfully asserted as a defense against the charge of violating § 922(g) (8), then the issue would be cloaked with legal significance. As it stands, it makes no difference.

...

And whatever the scope of the claimed Second Amendment right, no responsible individual or organization would suggest that it would protect Emerson's possession of the other guns found in his military-style arsenal the day the federal indictment was handed down. In addition to the Beretta nine millimeter pistol at issue here, Emerson had a second Beretta like the first, a semi-automatic M-1 carbine, an SKS assault rifle with bayonet, and a semi-automatic M-14 assault rifle. Nor would anyone suggest that Emerson's claimed right to keep and bear arms supercedes that of his wife, their daughter, and of others to be free from bodily harm or threats of harm.

...

If the majority was only filling the Federal Reporter with page after page of non-binding dicta there would be no need for me to write separately. As I have said, nothing in this case turns on the original meaning of the Second Amendment, so no court need follow what the majority has said in that regard. Unfortunately, however, the majority's exposition pertains to one of the most hotly-contested issues of the day. By overreaching in the area of Second Amendment law, the majority stirs this controversy without necessity when prudence and respect for stare decisis calls for it to say nothing at all.

The appellate court did discuss in this case that the Second Amendment protects an individual right, however, it did not go so far as to say that the individual right to gun ownership cannot be infringed upon. Rather they concluded that it is not an absolute right and is thus subject to government regulation. The law in question did not contradict the Second Amendment.

It's also interesting to note that while the overall decision in this case was agreed upon by the judges, the interpretation of the Second Amendment was not.

Silveira v. Lockyer — 2002

In 2002 a case made it to the US Court of Appeals for the Ninth Circuit which was a challenge to the constitutionality of the Roberti-Roos Assault Weapons Control Act of 1989, which was a California law that bans the ownership and transfer of specific brands and models of firearms classified as assault weapons. It was the first legislative restriction on assault weapons in the United States.

The plaintiffs claimed that the law violated the Second Amendment among other constitutional provisions, and the district court disagreed.

Judge Reinhardt, writing the opinion for the US Court of Appeals for the Ninth Circuit, recognized that there was a lot of new debate over the meaning of the Second Amendment, due to the increase in gun violence in the country. He proposed that there were three principal schools of thought around the meaning and purpose of the Second Amendment.

1. "Traditional individual rights" – *"the Second Amendment guarantees to individual private citizens a fundamental right to possess and use firearms for any purpose at all, subject only to limited government regulation. This view, urged by the NRA and other firearms enthusiasts, as well as by a prolific cadre of fervent supporters in the legal academy, had never been adopted by any court until the recent Fifth Circuit decision in United States v. Emerson"*
2. "Limited individual rights" – *"individuals maintain a constitutional right to possess firearms insofar as such possession bears a reasonable relationship to militia service."*
3. "Collective rights" – *"the federal and state governments have the full authority to enact prohibitions and restrictions on the use and possession of firearms, subject only to generally applicable constitutional constraints,*

such as due process, equal protection, and the like. Long the dominant view of the Second Amendment, and widely accepted by the federal courts, the collective rights model has recently come under strong criticism from individual rights advocates."

After analyzing the Second Amendment, its history, and its purpose, the court concluded that it is the collective rights model that is the most accurate.

Judge Reinhardt goes on to say that the most extensive treatment of the Second Amendment in previous Supreme Court cases was United States v Miller, which indicated that the Supreme Court rejected the traditional individual rights view. He also mentions Lewis v. United States which also rejected the traditional individual rights view.

Judge Reinhardt recognized that Justice Clarence Thomas may support the traditional individual rights view based on his dissent of the Printz v. United States decision before breaking down the meaning of the Second Amendment in detail.

The word "Militia", he says, is defined as "a state military entity, not to the people of the state as a whole." To confirm this, he points to how the word militia is used in the first and second articles of the US Constitution, and that it's apparent that the Framers were talking about state militias which were organized and primarily controlled by the state governments. The Fifth Amendment which has an exception for those in service of the militia uses the term in the same way.

The Fifth Amendment: *"No person shall be held to answer for a capital, or otherwise infamous crime, unless on a presentment or indictment of a grand jury, except in cases arising in the land or naval forces, or in the militia, when in actual service in time of war or public danger; nor shall any person be subject for the same offense to be twice put in jeopardy of life or limb; nor shall be compelled in any criminal case to be a witness against himself, nor be deprived of life, liberty, or property, without due process of law; nor shall private property be taken for public use, without just compensation."*

He also points out that the Articles of Confederation, the precursor to the US Constitution, used the term militia in the same way. In Judge Reinhardt's view:

To determine that "militia" in the Second Amendment is something different from the state entity referred to whenever that word is employed in the rest of the Constitution would be to apply contradictory interpretive methods to words in the same provision.

He concludes with two more points. First, the reading of the term militia meaning a state military force is supported by it being "necessary to the security of a free State" and by the fact that it has "well regulated" as a modifier – which makes it clear that the militia isn't just anyone.

After establishing the meaning of the first clause, and the term "militia", he moves on to the meaning of the rest of the amendment. He points out that "bear arms" is a phrase that is typically used in a military sense. He quotes the Tennessee Supreme Court in Aymette v. State (1840) where they said "*A man in pursuit of deer, elk and buffaloes might carry his rifle every day for forty years, and yet it would never be said of him that he had borne arms.*" He also quotes the Oxford English Dictionary which defined "to bear arms" as "*to serve as a soldier, do military service, fight.*"

There is more ambiguity, in Judge Reinhardt's view, of why the word "keep" exists in the Second Amendment, but he points out that there's little logic to the US v. Emerson decision indicating that it referred to keeping arms for personal use. The most likely reason is that the Framers meant for "keep" to be taken in a broader scope, as any other explanation would have both logical and historical difficulty. In other words, the militia needs to be able to possess the arms necessary for military effectiveness.

In 2021 the Roberti-Roos Assault Weapons Control Act of 1989 was overturned in Miller v. Bonta based on later Supreme Court decisions changing the way the Second Amendment is interpreted and applied.

Logan v. United States — 2007

In this case, Logan was found guilty of being a felon in possession of a firearm and was sentenced to fifteen years for it, because he had three relevant state convictions. After pleading guilty, he claimed that his civil rights were violated because his prior convictions did not result in the loss of his civil rights. His argument specifically referenced the law which said that a prior conviction may be disregarded if it's been expunged, or set aside, or if the offender has been pardoned or had his civil rights restored. He was arguing for a lesser sentence, saying that those prior convictions should not have been taken into account for his sentencing for this crime.

He took this argument to the United States Court of Appeals for the Seventh Circuit, which ruled against him, so he took it to the Supreme Court.

Ruth Bader Ginsburg

US Court of Appeals for the D.C. Circuit
1980-1993

Supreme Court of the United States
1993-2020

Courtesy Wikimedia Commons

Justice Ginsberg wrote the unanimous opinion primarily based on the Federal Law that Logan was accused of breaking (the Armed Career Criminal Act of 1984), not having a provision that handled his situation. She provided a detailed review of how that law and similar Federal and State laws interact.

She warns that treating the phrase "restored" as "retained" while interpreting the law would lead to illogical results and that the law should be read with the understanding that "civil rights restored" does not cover a person whose civil rights were never taken away. The judgment of the Court of Appeals for the Seventh Circuit was affirmed.

The decision was not based on any interpretation of the Second Amendment. However, the fact that it wasn't based on the Second Amendment goes against the interpretation where the individual right to own a gun cannot be abridged as his inability to possess a gun in the first place due to being a felon was not challenged.

D.C. v. Heller — 2008

In 2002 a senior fellow at the Cato Institute began shopping around for a case to challenge the Court's precedent on the Second Amendment in court. Even though he'd never owned a gun, he wanted to accomplish something like Thurgood Marshall did when school segregation was overturned. Thus, he sought out a diverse group of plaintiffs to put the question about an individual's right to bear arms before the courts and challenge the Firearm Control Regulations Act of 1975.

The case was first dismissed in a D.C. court, but it gained a 2–1 supporting decision in The Court of Appeals before reaching the Supreme Court.

The Supreme Court majority opinion held that yes, the Second Amendment did support an individual right to possess a firearm unconnected with service in a militia, making it the first decision by the Supreme Court in its 218 years to support the Individual Rights Theory.

Antonin Scalia

US Court of Appeals for the D.C. Circuit
1982-1986

Supreme Court of the United States
1986-2016

Courtesy Wikimedia Commons

Justice Scalia, writing a majority opinion that resembles the writings of David I. Caplan, goes with the Second Amendment being two separate parts rather than one coherent sentence:

The Second Amendment is naturally divided into two parts: its prefatory clause and its operative clause. The former does not limit the latter grammatically, but rather announces a purpose. The Amendment could be rephrased, "Because a well regulated Militia is necessary to the security of a free State, the right of the people to keep and bear Arms shall not be infringed." See J. Tiffany, A Treatise on Government and Constitutional Law §585, p. 394 (1867); Brief for Professors of Linguistics and English as Amici Curiae 3 (hereinafter Linguists' Brief). Although this structure of the Second Amendment is unique in our Constitution, other legal documents of the founding era, particularly individual-rights provisions of state constitutions, commonly included a prefatory statement of purpose. See generally Volokh, The Commonplace Second Amendment, 73 N. Y. U. L. Rev. 793, 814–821 (1998).

He breaks down the sentence into even smaller parts, trying to make the case that they mean something different when inspected closely. The "Right of the People," when used in other instances within the US Constitution, speaks of "individual rights" rather than "collective rights." Therefore, we can ignore the context of the Second Amendment and apply the context of those other instances instead. He does acknowledge that "the people" is used collectively. Still, he dismisses that usage because those instances do not mention a "right." (Note that the position of the Supreme Court at that time still proposed that the right to a militia is an Individual right, not a Collective right).

He then builds on this starting point:

Reading the Second Amendment as protecting only the right to "keep and bear Arms" in an organized militia therefore fits poorly with the operative clause's description of the holder of that right as "the people."

We start therefore with a strong presumption that the Second Amendment right is exercised individually and belongs to all Americans.

Moving on to "Keep and bear Arms," Justice Scalia breaks this down into "keep", "bare" and "arms" separately rather than as a whole phrase referencing the military organization of armed forces in uniform.

Before addressing the verbs "keep" and "bear," we interpret their object: "Arms." The 18th-century meaning is no different from the meaning today. The 1773 edition of Samuel Johnson's dictionary defined "arms" as "weapons of offence, or armour of defence." 1 Dictionary of the English Language 107 (4th ed.) (hereinafter Johnson). Timothy Cunningham's important 1771 legal dictionary defined "arms" as "any thing that a man wears for his defence, or takes into his hands, or useth in wrath to cast at or strike another." 1 A New and Complete Law Dictionary (1771); see also N. Webster, American Dictionary of the English Language (1828) (reprinted 1989) (hereinafter Webster) (similar).

He points out that the term Arms "applied, then as now, to weapons that were not specifically designed for military use and were not employed in a military capacity" – trying to define it apart from any context provided by the Second Amendment. Then, he pivots the argument to types of arms *"Some have made the argument, bordering on the frivolous, that only those arms in existence in the 18th century are protected by the Second Amendment."* He isn't clear on who those making that argument were, as no Supreme Court case at this point had ever determined that the type of arms was relevant to the Second Amendment. The closest thing was United States v. Miller which used the type of weapon to indicate that Miller and his companions were not in the well-regulated militia.

In defining "bear," he does acknowledge that when paired with "arms" it could change the meaning to one *"that refers to carrying for a particular purpose—confrontation."* He praises Justice Ginsburg, who wrote the Muscarello v. United States case he was referencing, saying that she *"accurately captured the natural meaning of "bear arms.""* before he made the following statement:

Although the phrase implies that the carrying of the weapon is for the purpose of "offensive or defensive action," it in no way connotes participation in a structured military organization.

Remember that Muscarello v. United States was NOT related to the Second Amendment. It was based on whether a federal law that used the phrase "uses or carries a firearm" applies to when that firearm is in a vehicle. It is doubtful that Justice Ginsburg would agree with Justice Scalia's interpretation of the Second Amendment, or else she would have mentioned it in Muscarello v. United States.

He also spends a lot of time disagreeing with the common interpretation of the United States v. Miller decision and directly how Justice Stevens interpreted it, saying:

a. "Well-Regulated Militia." In United States v. Miller, 307 U. S. 174, 179 (1939), we explained that "the Militia comprised all males physically capable of acting in concert for the common defense." That definition comports with founding-era sources.

However, he leaves out the next line which was ""*A body of citizens enrolled for military discipline.*"", and that the court ruled that Miller's Second Amendment Rights were not infringed upon.

Returning to what Justice Scalia said in D.C. v. Heller, despite having just made an argument to the contrary, he says that he agrees that "militia" means the same thing in Article 1 and the Second Amendment. He says, "*we believe that petitioners identify the wrong thing, namely, the organized militia.*" Thus, he's saying that the "*the state- and congressionally-regulated military forces described in the Militia Clauses* " are NOT the organized militia as per US Law. He says that Congress's power is to call forth an existing militia, not create a new one. He says both refer to "all able-bodied men" rather than well-regulated or organized. Here's his statement on this:

> *Petitioners take a seemingly narrower view of the militia, stating that "[m]ilitias are the state- and congressionally-regulated military forces described in the Militia Clauses (art. I, §8, cls. 15–16)." Brief for Petitioners 12. Although we agree with petitioners' interpretive assumption that "militia" means the same thing in Article I and the Second Amendment, we believe that petitioners identify the wrong thing, namely, the organized militia. Unlike armies and navies, which Congress is given the power to create ("to raise ... Armies"; "to provide ... a Navy," Art. I, §8, cls. 12–13), the militia is assumed by Article I already to be in existence. Congress is given the power to "provide for calling forth the militia," §8, cl. 15; and the power not to create, but to "organiz[e]" it—and not to organize "a" militia, which is what one would expect if the militia were to be a federal creation, but to organize "the" militia, connoting a body already in existence, ibid., cl. 16. This is fully consistent with the ordinary definition of the militia as all able-bodied men. From that pool, Congress has plenary power to organize the units that will make up an effective fighting force. That is what Congress did in the first militia Act, which specified that "each and every free able-bodied white male citizen of the respective states, resident therein, who is or shall be of the age of eighteen years, and under the age of forty-five years (except as is herein after excepted) shall severally and respectively be enrolled in the militia." Act of May 8, 1792, 1 Stat. 271. To be sure, Congress need not conscript every able-bodied man into the militia, because nothing in Article I suggests that in exercising its power to organize, discipline, and arm the militia, Congress must focus upon the entire body. Although the militia consists of all able-bodied men, the federally organized militia may consist of a subset of them.*

Of course, that interpretation makes "well regulated" completely meaningless, so he promptly dismisses it:

> *Finally, the adjective "well-regulated" implies nothing more than the imposition of proper discipline and training.*

Imposition means to impose an action or process, such

as requiring the state militia to be properly disciplined and trained. Perhaps by "nothing more" he was trying to separate the "well regulated militia" in the Second Amendment from the explanation of how the militia is to be kept disciplined and trained in Article 1 Section 8.

At this point, Justice Scalia's most significant problem in trying to make the Second Amendment match his new interpretation is that it says "for the security of a free State." An earlier draft of the Second Amendment said "free country," but it was changed to "free State" to clarify who the militia reported to, and "free country" had been shrunk down from "the military should be under strict subordination to, and governed by, the civil power." Justice Scalia takes advantage of the sparse wording to imply that State meant something other than a State in the Union, as it was being used artfully:

> "Security of a Free State." The phrase "security of a free state" meant "security of a free polity," not security of each of the several States as the dissent below argued, see 478 F. 3d, at 405, and n. 10. Joseph Story wrote in his treatise on the Constitution that "the word 'state' is used in various senses [and in] its most enlarged sense, it means the people composing a particular nation or community."
>
> …
>
> It is true that the term "State" elsewhere in the Constitution refers to individual States, but the phrase "security of a free state" and close variations seem to have been terms of art in 18th-century political discourse, meaning a " 'free country' " or free polity.

Contradictorily, Justice Scalia also says "the right to keep and bear arms" is silly to think of as an artful phrase, calling out Justice Stevens for saying so:

> Justice Stevens suggests that "keep and bear Arms" was some sort of term of art, presumably akin to "hue and cry" or "cease and desist." (This suggestion usefully evades the problem that there is no evidence whatsoever to support a military reading of "keep

arms.") Justice Stevens believes that the unitary meaning of "keep and bear Arms" is established by the Second Amendment's calling it a "right" (singular) rather than "rights" (plural). See post, at 16. There is nothing to this.

and that "the people" must mean the same thing throughout the US Constitution:

State constitutions of the founding period routinely grouped multiple (related) guarantees under a singular "right," and the First Amendment protects the "right [singular] of the people peaceably to assemble, and to petition the Government for a redress of grievances."

He then tries to dismiss the entirety of "A well regulated militia, necessary to the security of a free State" by saying there could be many different reasons a militia may be considered necessary.

There are many reasons why the militia was thought to be "necessary to the security of a free state." See 3 Story §1890. First, of course, it is useful in repelling invasions and suppressing insurrections. Second, it renders large standing armies unnecessary —an argument that Alexander Hamilton made in favor of federal control over the militia. The Federalist No. 29, pp. 226, 227 (B. Wright ed. 1961) (A. Hamilton). Third, when the able-bodied men of a nation are trained in arms and organized, they are better able to resist tyranny.

While Alexander Hamilton, in Federalist 29, did say, "This desirable uniformity can only be accomplished by confiding the regulation of the militia to the direction of the national authority. It is, therefore, with the most evident propriety, that the plan of the convention proposes to empower the Union 'to provide for organizing, arming, and disciplining the militia, and for governing such part of them as may be employed in the service of the United States, RESERVING TO THE STATES RESPECTIVELY THE APPOINTMENT OF THE OFFICERS, AND

THE AUTHORITY OF TRAINING THE MILITIA ACCORDING TO THE DISCIPLINE PRESCRIBED BY CONGRESS." it's not accurate to say that the entirety of the essay favored federal control over the militia. Alexander Hamilton pointed out the flaw of that argument:

What reason could there be to infer, that force was intended to be the sole instrument of authority, merely because there is a power to make use of it when necessary? What shall we think of the motives which could induce men of sense to reason in this manner? How shall we prevent a conflict between charity and judgment?

Justice Scalia continues to say:

What reasonable cause of apprehension can be inferred from a power in the Union to prescribe regulations for the militia, and to command its services when necessary, while the particular States are to have the SOLE AND EXCLUSIVE APPOINTMENT OF THE OFFICERS? If it were possible seriously to indulge a jealousy of the militia upon any conceivable establishment under the federal government, the circumstance of the officers being in the appointment of the States ought at once to extinguish it. There can be no doubt that this circumstance will always secure to them a preponderating influence over the militia.

It's clear that Justice Scalia is trying to separate the militia described in the Second Amendment from the militia Alexander Hamilton was discussing while he was promoting the Article 1 Section 8 power of Congress "to provide for organizing, arming, and disciplining" them. However, Alexander Hamilton argued that the militia being discussed in Article 1 Section 8 was a State militia while not deemed necessary to call them into federal service.

After Justice Scalia has separated the Second Amendment into unrelated pieces, he discusses the relationship between the "prefatory" clause and the "operative" clause.

It is therefore entirely sensible that the Second Amendment's prefatory clause announces the purpose for which the right was codified: to prevent elimination of the militia. The prefatory clause does not suggest that preserving the militia was the only reason Americans valued the ancient right; most undoubtedly thought it even more important for self-defense and hunting. But the threat that the new Federal Government would destroy the citizens' militia by taking away their arms was the reason that right—unlike some other English rights—was codified in a written Constitution. Justice Breyer's assertion that individual self-defense is merely a "subsidiary interest" of the right to keep and bear arms, see post, at 36, is profoundly mistaken. He bases that assertion solely upon the prologue—but that can only show that self-defense had little to do with the right's codification; it was the central component of the right itself.

While he's correct that Americans did value their ability to own firearms, the idea that it was "entirely sensible" for that to have been the topic of the Second Amendment is not backed by the record of the Debates of Several States on the topic.

As he goes on, at one point, he says that the English Bill of Rights included a "right to bear arms." The following is the only mention of "arms" in the English Bill of Rights:

That the subjects which are Protestants may have arms for their defence suitable to their conditions and as allowed by law;

That is not comparable to the wording in the Second Amendment. It is about self-defense, not the common defense of a free State, and it says "as allowed by law" which renders the sentence powerless to prevent laws from abridging the right to have arms.

What Justice Scalia was quoting is the Commentaries on the Constitution of the United States, from 1833 by Justice Joseph Story. He references section 1858, which is:

Sec. 1858. In the next place, a bill of rights is important, and may often be indispensable, whenever it operates, as a qualification upon powers, actually granted by the people to the government. This is the real ground of all the bills of rights in the parent country, in the colonial constitutions and laws, and in the state constitutions. In England, the bills of rights were not demanded merely of the Crown, as withdrawing a power from the royal prerogative; they were equally important, as withdrawing power from parliament. A large proportion of the most valuable of the provisions in Magna Charta, and the bill of rights in 1688, consists of a solemn recognition, of limitations upon the power of parliament; that is, a declaration, that parliament ought not to abolish, or restrict those rights. Such are the right of trial by jury; the right to personal liberty and private property according to the law of the land; that the subjects ought to have a right to bear arms; that elections of members of parliament ought to be free; that freedom of speech and debate in parliament ought not to be impeached, or questioned elsewhere; and that excessive bail ought not to be required, nor excessive fines imposed, nor cruel or unusual punishments inflicted. Whenever, then, a general power exists, or is granted to a government, which may in its actual exercise or abuse be dangerous to the people, there seems a peculiar propriety in restricting its operations, and in excepting from it some at least of the most mischievous forms, in which it may be likely to be abused. And the very exception in such cases will operate with a silent, but irresistible influence to control the actual abuse of it in other analogous cases.

In that text, Joseph Story describes the importance of having a bill of rights – he's not specifically talking about the Second Amendment. In the later sections, Justice Story explains that the Second Amendment is about the well-regulated militia (Recall that he said having a well-regulated militia over a standing army provides a moral check against tyranny).

To counter what Joseph Story said in Sec. 1891 about the provision mentioned in the English Bill of Rights being "more nominal than real", Justice Scalia says:

This comparison to the Declaration of Right would not make sense if the Second Amendment right was the right to use a gun in a militia, which was plainly not what the English right protected.

Since the opposing argument is that the Second Amendment is about the State having power over the State Militia rather than the Federal Government (except when necessary), his point about "the right to use a gun in a militia" is unrelated to the topic.

He also mentions that in Houston v. Moore, the Supreme Court held that the States have concurrent power over the militia. Rather than quoting the majority opinion, Justice Scalia quotes the dissent (written by Justice Joseph Story):

The 19th-century cases that interpreted the Second Amendment universally support an individual right unconnected to militia service. In Houston v. Moore, 5 Wheat. 1, 24 (1820), this Court held that States have concurrent power over the militia, at least where not pre-empted by Congress. Agreeing in dissent that States could "organize, discipline, and arm" the militia in the absence of conflicting federal regulation, Justice Story said that the Second Amendment "may not, perhaps, be thought to have any important bearing on this point. If it have, it confirms and illustrates, rather than impugns the reasoning already suggested." Id., at 51–53. Of course, if the Amendment simply "protect[ed] the right of the people of each of the several States to maintain a well-regulated militia," post, at 1 (Stevens, J., dissenting), it would have enormous and obvious bearing on the point. But the Court and Story derived the States' power over the militia from the nonexclusive nature of federal power, not from the Second Amendment, whose preamble merely "confirms and illustrates" the importance of the militia. Even clearer was Justice Baldwin. In the famous fugitive-slave case of Johnson v. Tompkins, 13 F. Cas. 840, 850, 852 (CC Pa. 1833), Baldwin, sitting as a circuit judge, cited both the Second Amendment and the Pennsylvania analogue for his conclusion that a citizen has "a right to carry arms in defence of his property or person, and to use them, if either were assailed with such force, numbers or violence as made it necessary for the protection or safety of either."

Recall that Houston v. Moore was not a case deciding if anyone's individual Second Amendment rights were being infringed; it was a case trying a militia man who had disobeyed the call of the President. It was about the militia clauses of Article 1 Section 8. When we look at a larger quote from Joseph Story's argument (provided in the earlier chapter on Houston v. Moore), it's clear that he wasn't saying that the Second Amendment supported an individual right unconnected to militia service. Joseph Story was talking about how Congress's power over the militia was limited not only by the Second Amendment but also by Article 1 Section 8.

Justice Story's viewpoint was that "the states, in virtue of their sovereignty, possessed general authority over their own militia" and that they should be able to "call forth its own militia" and this is what the Second Amendment "confirms, and illustrates, not that it is about "an individual right unconnected to militia service." When he says "confirms and illustrates," he's saying that the Second Amendment backs up Article 1 Section 8 rather than contradicts it. The reason he dissented in that case was because he felt that States should enforce State laws, and the Federal government should enforce Federal laws.

Justice Scalia also claimed that the United States v. Cruikshank decision supports his interpretation of the Second Amendment because there was a lack of discussion. *"The limited discussion of the Second Amendment in Cruikshank supports, if anything, the individual-rights interpretation. There was no claim in Cruikshank that the victims had been deprived of their right to carry arms in a militia; indeed, the Governor had disbanded the local militia unit the year before the mob's attack, see C. Lane, The Day Freedom Died 62 (2008)."*

He then mentions Presser v. Illinois, saying that because it was about military organizations and drilling or parading with arms in cities, that does not refute his interpretation either.

He completely dismisses the Presser v. Illinois decision in any interpretation of the Second Amendment: *"Presser said nothing about the Second Amendment's meaning or scope, beyond the fact that it does not prevent the prohibition of private paramilitary organizations."*

What Presser upheld is that the Second Amendment's scope is "only upon the power of Congress and the national government and not upon that of the state" – so it does provide clarity of scope and meaning of the Second Amendment. Presser *"was not a member of the organized volunteer militia of the State of Illinois, nor did he belong to the troops of the United States or to any organization under the militia law of the United States. On the contrary, the fact that he did not belong to the organized militia or the troops of the United States was an ingredient in the offense for which he was convicted and sentenced."* – the Second Amendment did not apply to the plaintiff because he wasn't a member of a militia recognized by the U.S. Constitution.

Justice Scalia moves on to the Miller decision, indicating that most arguments that oppose his new interpretation come primarily from United States v. Miller:

Justice Stevens places overwhelming reliance upon this Court's decision in United States v. Miller, 307 U. S. 174 (1939). "[H]undreds of judges," we are told, "have relied on the view of the amendment we endorsed there," post, at 2, and "[e]ven if the textual and historical arguments on both side of the issue were evenly balanced, respect for the well-settled views of all of our predecessors on this Court, and for the rule of law itself ... would prevent most jurists from endorsing such a dramatic upheaval in the law," post, at 4. And what is, according to Justice Stevens, the holding of Miller that demands such obeisance? That the Second Amendment "protects the right to keep and bear arms for certain military purposes, but that it does not curtail the legislature's power to regulate the nonmilitary use and ownership of weapons." Post, at 2.

Nothing so clearly demonstrates the weakness of Justice Stevens' case. Miller did not hold that and cannot possibly be read to have held that. The judgment in the case upheld against a Second Amendment challenge two men's federal convictions for transporting an unregistered short-barreled shotgun in interstate commerce, in violation of the National Firearms Act, 48 Stat. 1236. It is entirely clear that the Court's basis for saying that the Second Amendment did not apply was not that the defendants were "bear[ing] arms" not "for ... military purposes" but for "nonmilitary use," post, at 2. Rather, it was that the type of weapon at issue was not eligible for Second Amendment protection: "In the absence of any evidence tending to show that the possession or use of a [short-barreled shotgun] at this time has some reasonable relationship to the preservation or efficiency of a well regulated militia, we cannot say that the Second Amendment guarantees the right to keep and bear such an instrument." 307 U. S., at 178 (emphasis added). "Certainly," the Court continued, "it is not within judicial notice that this weapon is any part of the ordinary military equipment or that its use could contribute to the common defense." Ibid. Beyond that, the opinion provided no explanation of the content of the right.

According to Justice Scalia, not only did the court fail to explain the Second Amendment when Presser claimed his Second Amendment rights were infringed, but they failed again with Miller made the same accusation.

It is particularly wrongheaded to read Miller for more than what it said, because the case did not even purport to be a thorough examination of the Second Amendment.

Once again, let's review what the Court said in United States v. Miller:

In the absence of any evidence tending to show that possession or use of a "shotgun having a barrel of less than eighteen inches in length" at this time has some reasonable relationship to the preservation or efficiency of a well regulated militia, we cannot say that the Second Amendment guarantees the right to keep and bear such an instrument. Certainly it is not within judicial notice that this weapon is any part of the ordinary military equipment, or that its use could contribute to the common defense. Aymette v. State, 2 Humphreys (Tenn.) 154, 158.

The Constitution, as originally adopted, granted to the Congress power --

"To provide for calling forth the Militia to execute the Laws of the Union, suppress Insurrections and repel Invasions; To provide for organizing, arming, and disciplining, the Militia, and for governing such Part of them as may be employed in the Service of the United States, reserving to the States respectively, the Appointment of the Officers, and the Authority of training the Militia according to the discipline prescribed by Congress."

With obvious purpose to assure the continuation and render possible the effectiveness of such forces, the declaration and guarantee of the Second Amendment were made. It must be interpreted and applied with that end in view.

The Miller decision did explain the nature of the right in the Second Amendment; it said that the right must be interpreted and applied in the context of calling forth the Militia to execute the law, suppress insurrections, and repel invasions. About the Miller decision about the Second Amendment having to be interpreted with that end in view, Justice Scalia says:

This holding is not only consistent with, but positively suggests, that the Second Amendment confers an individual right to keep and bear arms (though only arms that "have some reasonable relationship to the preservation or efficiency of a well regulated militia"). Had the Court believed that the Second Amendment protects only those serving in the militia, it would have been odd to examine the character of the weapon rather than simply note that the two crooks were not militiamen.

He says that interpreting the Miller decision as supporting

The Collective Rights Theory is wrong... because they didn't make some other argument he would have. He concludes his discussion of Miller with:

We therefore read Miller to say only that the Second Amendment does not protect those weapons not typically possessed by law-abiding citizens for lawful purposes, such as short-barreled shotguns. That accords with the historical understanding of the scope of the right

Despite the ruling going against precedence, the Supreme Court in this case did not rule that all gun control laws were unconstitutional. Shooting down the most extreme interpretations of the interpretation. Justice Scalia says:

Like most rights, the right secured by the Second Amendment is not unlimited. From Blackstone through the 19th-century cases, commentators and courts routinely explained that the right was not a right to keep and carry any weapon whatsoever in any manner whatsoever and for whatever purpose. See, e.g., Sheldon, in 5 Blume 346; Rawle 123; Pomeroy 152–153; Abbott 333.

He also says:

We also recognize another important limitation on the right to keep and carry arms. Miller said, as we have explained, that the sorts of weapons protected were those "in common use at the time." 307 U. S., at 179. We think that limitation is fairly supported by the historical tradition of prohibiting the carrying of "dangerous and unusual weapons."

He continues with the theme of making half of the Second Amendment irrelevant by saying that sometimes the right specified in the Second Amendment is "completely detached from the prefatory clause":

It may be objected that if weapons that are most useful in military service—M-16 rifles and the like—may be banned, then the Second Amendment right is completely detached from the prefatory clause.

But as we have said, the conception of the militia at the time of the Second Amendment's ratification was the body of all citizens capable of military service, who would bring the sorts of lawful weapons that they possessed at home to militia duty. It may well be true today that a militia, to be as effective as militias in the 18th century, would require sophisticated arms that are highly unusual in society at large. Indeed, it may be true that no amount of small arms could be useful against modern-day bombers and tanks. But the fact that modern developments have limited the degree of fit between the prefatory clause and the protected right cannot change our interpretation of the right.

Moving on to discussing the District of Columbia law the court was reviewing; he focuses on the idea that the Second Amendment is about self-defense rather than the common defense.

We must also address the District's requirement (as applied to respondent's handgun) that firearms in the home be rendered and kept inoperable at all times. This makes it impossible for citizens to use them for the core lawful purpose of self-defense and is hence unconstitutional.

He provides a summary of the decision:

In sum, we hold that the District's ban on handgun possession in the home violates the Second Amendment, as does its prohibition against rendering any lawful firearm in the home operable for the purpose of immediate self-defense. Assuming that Heller is not disqualified from the exercise of Second Amendment rights, the District must permit him to register his handgun and must issue him a license to carry it in the home.

After the summary, he takes the opportunity to dismiss the idea that the Second Amendment is outdated:

Undoubtedly some think that the Second Amendment is outmoded in a society where our standing army is the pride of our Nation, where well-trained police forces provide personal security, and where gun violence is a serious problem. That is perhaps debatable, but what is not debatable is that it is not the role of this Court to pronounce the Second Amendment extinct.

Justice Scalia's approach was perhaps flawed not only because he said that the Second Amendment only protected individuals' right to keep and carry arms, but also because he implied that was the initial purpose when the debates that led to the writing of the Second Amendment were clearly about the well-regulated militia.

The court's decision was far from unanimous, as the four dissenting Justices (out of nine) wrote two dissenting opinions, with all four joining both dissents. Neither of the dissents made the argument that the Second Amendment was old-fashioned, should be pronounced extinct, that it does not cover an individual right, or that it was about only the militia being able to keep and bear arms.

John Paul Stevens

United States Navy 1942-1945

US Court of Appeals for the Seventh Circuit 1970-1975

Supreme Court of the United States 1975-2010

Justice Stevens explained what the Second Amendment was for:

The Second Amendment was adopted to protect the right of the people of each of the several States to maintain a well-regulated militia. It was a response to concerns raised during the ratification of the Constitution that the power of Congress to disarm the state militias and create a national standing army posed an intolerable threat to the sovereignty of the several States. Neither the text of the Amendment nor the arguments advanced by its proponents evidenced the slightest interest in limiting any legislature's authority to regulate private civilian uses of firearms. Specifically, there is no indication that the Framers of the Amendment intended to enshrine the common-law right of self-defense in the Constitution.

He called the majority opinion unpersuasive and a dramatic upheaval in the law, saying that it is "abundantly clear that the Amendment should not be interpreted as limiting the authority of Congress to regulate the use or possession of firearms for purely civilian purposes." He also pointed out that the Second Amendment did not include any statement of purpose for the right to firearms for hunting or personal self-defense, which was present in other Declarations of Rights such as for Pennsylvania and Vermont. The Stevens dissent had four main points:

1. "to keep and bear arms" was on military uses of firearms, which [the Framers] viewed in the context of service in state militias

2. the "right to keep and bear arms" protects only a right to possess and use firearms in connection with service in a state-organized militia

3. stare decisis (standing by previous court decisions) was established by Miller and all lower court interpretations of it (and the Majority opinion went against stare decisis)

4. the Courts have not considered gun-control laws unconstitutional.

Stephen Breyer

United States Army 1957-1965

US Court of Appeals for the First Circuit 1980-1994

Supreme Court of the United States 1994-2022

In the second dissent, written by Justice Breyer, he says:

The majority's conclusion is wrong for two independent reasons. The first reason is that set forth by Justice Stevens — namely, that the Second Amendment protects militia-related, not self-defense-related, interests. These two interests are sometimes intertwined. To assure 18th-century citizens that they could keep arms for militia purposes would necessarily have allowed them to keep arms that they could have used for self-defense as well. But self-defense alone, detached from any militia-related objective, is not the Amendment's concern.

The second independent reason is that the protection the Amendment provides is not absolute. The Amendment permits government to regulate the interests that it serves. Thus, irrespective of what those interests are — whether they do or do not include an independent interest in self-defense — the majority's view cannot be correct unless it can show that the District's regulation is unreasonable or inappropriate in Second Amendment terms. This the majority cannot do.

He also spells out four propositions based on precedent and current opinions that he believed the entire Court subscribed to:

(1) The Amendment protects an "individual" right—i.e., one that is separately possessed, and may be separately enforced, by each

person on whom it is conferred. See, e.g., ante, at 22 (opinion of the Court); ante, at 1 (Stevens, J., dissenting).

(2) As evidenced by its preamble, the Amendment was adopted "[w]ith obvious purpose to assure the continuation and render possible the effectiveness of [militia] forces." United States v. Miller, 307 U. S. 174, 178 (1939); see ante, at 26 (opinion of the Court); ante, at 1 (Stevens, J., dissenting).

(3) The Amendment "must be interpreted and applied with that end in view." Miller, supra, at 178.

(4) The right protected by the Second Amendment is not absolute, but instead is subject to government regulation. See Robertson v. Baldwin, 165 U. S. 275, 281–282 (1897); ante, at 22, 54 (opinion of the Court).

After the Supreme Court ruling, Heller went back to the D.C. Circuit court to request that the court overturn the new gun ordinances enacted. After covering five different ways the lower courts had thus far tried to implement the Heller Decision, and evaluating the new laws, the D.C. Circuit ruled that the laws were not infringing upon anyone's Second Amendment rights.

McDonald v. Chicago — 2010

The DC v Heller not only overturned the historic court interpretations of the Second Amendment (stare decisis), but it also has the potential to invalidate existing laws. Chicago had a similar law to the one the Supreme Court struck down, but the people of Chicago and Oak Park argued that their laws were still constitutional because they were in a US State, unlike DC. They believed that the Second Amendment did not apply to the States as it is primarily a limitation on the Federal Government, not a limitation on State governments.

Samuel Alito

United States Army 1972-1980

US Court of Appeals for the Third Circuit 1990-2006

Supreme Court of the United States 2006 -

Courtesy Wikimedia Commons

The Supreme Court's decision, which reversed the decision by the Court of Appeals, declared that an individual right to "keep and bear arms" is incorporated by the Due Process Clause of the Fourteenth Amendment, which states:

No State shall make or enforce any law which shall abridge the privileges or immunities of citizens of the United States; nor shall any State deprive any person of life, liberty, or property, without due process of law; nor deny to any person within its jurisdiction the equal protection of the laws.

Justice Alito wrote the majority decision, emphasizing that

the Second Amendment concerns individual rights. Thus, any protections of individual rights that apply to the Federal Government also apply to the State Governments due to the incorporation doctrine.

This time there were two concurring opinions written by Justice Scalia and Justice Thomas. Justice Scalia focused on the incorporation doctrine, while Justice Thomas went into American history and the nation's founding and talked about how the right to bear arms exists outside of the Second Amendment.

Yet again, the decision was split, with four Justices dissenting, with Justices Breyer and Stevens each writing their own dissent.

Justice Stevens wrote:

The fact that the right to keep and bear arms appears in the Constitution should not obscure the novelty of the Court's decision to enforce that right against the States. By its terms, the Second Amendment does not apply to the States; read properly, it does not even apply to individuals outside of the militia context. The Second Amendment was adopted to protect the States from federal encroachment. And the Fourteenth Amendment has never been understood by the Court to have "incorporated" the entire Bill of Rights. There was nothing foreordained about today's outcome.

Justice Breyer wrapped up with the following:

In sum, the Framers did not write the Second Amendment in order to protect a private right of armed self-defense. There has been, and is, no consensus that the right is, or was, "fundamental." No broader constitutional interest or principle supports legal treatment of that right as fundamental. To the contrary, broader constitutional concerns of an institutional nature argue strongly against that treatment.

U.S. v. Marzzarella — 2010

In April of 2006, the Pennsylvania State Police were notified that Marzzarella was involved in the sale of stolen handguns. After an investigation and arrest, Marzzarella was arrested for possessing a firearm with an obliterated serial number violating Federal law. Marzzarella claimed that his Second Amendment right to keep and bear arms was being infringed. The case reached the United States Court of Appeals, Third Circuit. The District Court had previously denied Marzzarella's claim saying that the Second Amendment does not protect a right to own handguns with obliterated serial numbers and that the law doesn't burden the core right recognized in the Heller decision, which was the right to possess firearms for the defense of hearth and home. The District Court had also said that even if Marzzarella's possession of the pistol were protected by the Second Amendment, the law in question would still be a constitutionally permissible regulation of Second Amendment rights.

Anthony Joseph Scirica

Pennsylvania House of Representatives 1971-1980

US District Court for E.D. Pa. 1984-1987

US Court of Appeals for the Third Circuit 1987-

Courtesy Wikimedia Commons

The United States Court of Appeals, Third Circuit, in an opinion written by Judge Scirica, reviewed the Heller decision and provided a quick recap:

In Heller, the Supreme Court struck down several District of Columbia statutes prohibiting the possession of handguns and requiring lawfully owned firearms to be kept inoperable. 128 S.Ct. at 2817-18. The Court concluded the Second Amendment "confer[s] an individual right to keep and bear arms," id. at 2799, at least for the core purpose of allowing law-abiding citizens to "use arms in defense of hearth and home," id. at 2821. Although the Court declined to fully define the scope of the right to possess firearms, it did caution that the right is not absolute. Id. at 2816-17 ("Like most rights, the right secured by the Second Amendment is not unlimited. . . . [N]othing in our opinion should be taken to cast doubt on longstanding prohibitions on the possession of firearms. . . ."). But because the District of Columbia's laws prevented persons from possessing firearms even for self-defense in the home, they were unconstitutional under any form of means-end scrutiny applicable to assess the validity of limitations on constitutional rights. Id. at 2817-18 ("Under any of the standards of scrutiny that we have applied to enumerated constitutional rights . . . [the statutes] would fail constitutional muster." (citation and footnote omitted)).

Within the scope of how they understood the Heller decision, and First Amendment challenges, they establish a two-step approach to Second Amendment cases. Step one is to check if the law in question falls within the scope of the Second Amendment.

As we read Heller, it suggests a two-pronged approach to Second Amendment challenges. First, we ask whether the challenged law imposes a burden on conduct falling within the scope of the Second Amendment's guarantee. Cf. United States v. Stevens, 533 F.3d 218, 233 (3d Cir. 2008), aff'd ___ U.S. ___, 130 S.Ct. 1577, 176 L.Ed.2d 435 (recognizing the preliminary issue in a First Amendment challenge is whether the speech at issue is protected or unprotected). If it does not, our inquiry is complete. If it does, we evaluate the law under some form of means-end scrutiny. If the law passes muster under that standard, it is constitutional. If it fails, it is invalid.

They also point out some flaws in the new standards set by the Heller decision.

We recognize the phrase "presumptively lawful" could have different meanings under newly enunciated Second Amendment doctrine. On the one hand, this language could be read to suggest the identified restrictions are presumptively lawful because they regulate conduct outside the scope of the Second Amendment. On the other hand, it may suggest the restrictions are presumptively lawful because they pass muster under any standard of scrutiny. Both readings are reasonable interpretations, but we think the better reading, based on the text and the structure of Heller, is the former — in other words, that these longstanding limitations are exceptions to the right to bear arms. Immediately following the above-quoted passage, the Court discussed "another important limitation" on the Second Amendment — restrictions on the types of weapons individuals may possess. Heller, 128 S.Ct. at 2817.

Thus, they say that if the Second Amendment codified a pre-existing right to bear arms, then what it was codifying is the existing understanding of what that right was at the time – and there have been arms regulations and arms control laws in the U.S. going back to at least 1619. They also interpreted Heller as to say that felons and mentally ill are disqualified from exercising their Second Amendment Rights, and the same is true for laws about carrying firearms in sensitive places.

In this, the Court did not believe the law prevented Marzzarella's Second Amendment rights, as he would have been able to own a handgun where the serial numbers were still intact.

The second step, if the law does fall within the scope of the Second Amendment, is to evaluate the law under some form of means-end scrutiny. In this, they point out another incongruity between standard practices and the recommendations of the Heller decision.

The Government argues a rational basis test should apply to § 922(k), but Heller rejects that standard for laws burdening Second Amendment rights. Id. at 2816 n. 27. The Court noted that even a law as burdensome as the District of Columbia's handgun ban would be constitutional under a rational basis test. Id. The fact that the ban was struck down, therefore, indicates some form of heightened scrutiny must have applied. Moreover, "[i]f all that was required to overcome the right to keep and bear arms was a rational basis, the Second Amendment would be redundant with the separate constitutional prohibitions on irrational laws, and would have no effect." Id.

They expressly point out that Heller suggests an entirely different approach to Second Amendment challenges than the courts take with First Amendment challenges.

Whether or not strict scrutiny may apply to particular Second Amendment challenges, it is not the case that it must be applied to all Second Amendment challenges. Strict scrutiny does not apply automatically any time an enumerated right is involved. We do not treat First Amendment challenges that way. Strict scrutiny is triggered by content-based restrictions on speech in a public forum, see Pleasant Grove City v. Summum, ___ U.S. ___, ___, 129 S.Ct. 1125, 1132, 172 L.Ed.2d 853 (2009), but content-neutral time, place, and manner restrictions in a public forum trigger a form of intermediate scrutiny, see Ward v. Rock Against Racism, 491 U.S. 781, 791, 109 S.Ct. 2746, 105 L.Ed.2d 661 (1989) (upholding such restrictions if they "are justified without reference to the content of the regulated speech, . . . they are narrowly tailored to serve a significant governmental interest, and . . . they leave open ample alternative channels for communication of the information." (quoting Clark v. Cmty. for Creative Non-Violence, 468 U.S. 288, 293, 104 S.Ct. 3065, 82 L.Ed.2d 221 (1984))).

In sum, the right to free speech, an undeniably enumerated fundamental right, see W. Va. State Bd. of Educ. v. Barnette, 319 U.S. 624, 638, 63 S.Ct. 1178, 87 L.Ed. 1628 (1943), is susceptible to several standards of scrutiny, depending upon the type of law challenged and the type of speech at issue. We see no reason why the Second Amendment would be any different.

After their means-end scrutiny, they determined that the Pennsylvania law does not infringe upon the Second Amendment.

Because § 922(k) was neither designed to nor has the effect of prohibiting the possession of any class of firearms, it is more accurately characterized as a regulation of the manner in which persons may lawfully exercise their Second Amendment rights. The distinction between limitations on the exercise of protected conduct and regulation of the form in which that conduct occurs also appears in the First Amendment context.

Judge Scirica, for The United States Court of Appeals, Third Circuit, concludes by saying that Marzzarella's Second Amendment Rights were not infringed.

Second Amendment doctrine remains in its nascency, and lower courts must proceed deliberately when addressing regulations unmentioned by Heller. Accordingly, we hesitate to say Marzzarella's possession of an unmarked firearm in his home is unprotected conduct. But because § 922(k) would pass muster under either intermediate scrutiny or strict scrutiny, Marzzarella's conviction must stand.

For the foregoing reasons, we will affirm the District Court's denial of Marzzarella's motion to dismiss the indictment and affirm his judgment of conviction and sentence.

Moore v. Madigan — 2012

Two appeals were consolidated to challenge Illinois gun control laws under the Second Amendment. This challenge reached the United States Court of Appeals, Seventh Circuit. With a few exceptions, the Illinois law forbade people to carry guns that were loaded, immediately accessible, and ready to use outside their homes, fixed places of business, or on the property where the owner gave permission.

The majority opinion, written by Judge Posner, reads as if the Heller decision gave them no choice but to rule in a way opposite to how they would have before Heller.

We are disinclined to engage in another round of historical analysis to determine whether eighteenth-century America understood the Second Amendment to include a right to bear guns outside the home. The Supreme Court has decided that the amendment confers a right to bear arms for self-defense, which is as important outside the home as inside. The theoretical and empirical evidence (which overall is inconclusive) is consistent with concluding that a right to carry firearms in public may promote self-defense. Illinois had to provide us with more than merely a rational basis for believing that its uniquely sweeping ban is justified by an increase in public safety. It has failed to meet this burden. The Supreme Court's interpretation of the Second Amendment therefore compels us to reverse the decisions in the two cases before us and remand them to their respective district courts for the entry of declarations of unconstitutionality and permanent injunctions. Nevertheless we order our mandate stayed for 180 days to allow the Illinois legislature to craft a new gun law that will impose reasonable limitations, consistent with the public safety and the Second Amendment as interpreted in this opinion, on the carrying of guns in public.

Ann Claire Williams

US District Court for the N.D. of Illinois 1985-1999

US Court of Appeals for the Seventh Circuit 1999-2018

Courtesy Wikimedia Commons

Judge Williams filed a dissenting opinion, stating that Heller did not clarify if this new interpretation of a Second Amendment right to self-defense existed outside of the home, and in her view, *"Whether the Second Amendment protects a right to carry ready-to-use firearms in public for potential self-defense requires a different analysis from that conducted by the Court in Heller and McDonald."* She points out a flaw in the Heller decision, that Judges are not historians. She says:

The focus of Heller's historical examination was on whether the Second Amendment included an individual right to bear arms or whether that right was limited to militia service. Once the Heller majority found that the Second Amendment was personal, the conclusion that one could possess ready-to-use firearms in the home for self-defense there makes sense in light of the home-as-castle history.

It is less clear to me, however, that a widely understood right to carry ready-to-use arms in public for potential self-defense existed at the time of the founding.

She points out that the Supreme Court may have misinterpreted some of its references in Heller.

Some, like the plaintiffs, read Blackstone to mean that the Statute of Northampton was understood to cover only those circumstances where the carrying of arms was unusual and therefore terrifying. But that seems to be a strained reading of Blackstone's words. The more natural reading is that Blackstone states that riding or going armed with dangerous weapons is an offense and is a crime against the public peace. He then explains why the offense of riding or going armed with dangerous weapons is a crime against the public peace—because doing so makes people terrified or nervous. Notably, Blackstone compares going armed with dangerous weapons to the mere act of walking around a city in armor, which was prohibited in ancient Greece. The comparison suggests that just as seeing a person walking around a city in armor would cause other citizens to be nervous, regardless of any affirmative action, so would the reaction be to seeing another carrying dangerous weapons in a populated area.

She also points out that the Heller decision demonstrates that the right to carry a loaded gun outside the home is not a right guaranteed by the Second Amendment (something Justice Thomas disagrees with later).

I am not convinced that the implication of the Heller and McDonald decisions is that the Second Amendment right to have ready-to-use firearms for potential self-defense extends beyond the home. That the Second Amendment speaks of the "right of the people to keep and bear arms" (emphasis added) does not to me imply a right to carry a loaded gun outside the home. Heller itself demonstrates this. The Court interpreted "bear" to mean to "carry" or to "wear, bear, or carry," upon one's person, for the purpose of being armed and ready in case of conflict. Heller, 554 U.S. at 584, 128 S.Ct. 2783. And we know that Heller contemplated that a gun might only be carried in the home because it ordered the District of Columbia to permit Heller to do precisely that: it directed that unless Heller was otherwise disqualified, the District must allow him "to register his handgun and must issue him a license to carry it in the home." Id. at 635, 128 S.Ct. 2783 (emphasis added). Mr. Heller did not want simply "to keep" a gun in his closet. He wanted to be able "to bear" it in case of self-defense, and the Supreme Court said he could.

She continues with:

Any right to carry loaded firearms outside the home for self-defense is, under Heller's own terms, susceptible to a legislative determination that firearms should not be allowed in certain public places.

and explains that the Heller decision doesn't make sense:

It is difficult to make sense of what Heller means for carrying guns in public for another notable reason. Immediately before the sentence giving a presumption of lawfulness to bans on guns for felons and the like, Heller states: "Like most rights, the right secured by the Second Amendment is not unlimited. From Blackstone through the 19th-century cases, commentators and courts routinely explained that the right was not a right to keep and carry any weapon whatsoever in any manner whatsoever and for whatever purpose. For example, the majority of the 19th-century courts to consider the question held that prohibitions on carrying concealed weapons were lawful under the Second Amendment or state analogues." 554 U.S. at 626, 128 S.Ct. 2783 (emphasis added and internal citations omitted). The implication of the Supreme Court's statement would seem to be that concealed carry is not within the scope of the Second Amendment (or at the least that that is the presumption).

Judge Williams concludes her dissent by saying that in this case, what related laws exist in Illinois should be up to the State of Illinois.

Reasonable people can differ on how guns should be regulated. Illinois has chosen to prohibit most forms of public carry of ready-to-use guns. It reaffirmed that just last year, when its legislature considered and rejected a measure to permit persons to carry concealed weapons in Illinois. See Dave McKinney, Concealed-Carry Measure: Shot Down in Springfield, Chicago Sun–Times, 2011 WLNR 9215695 (May 6, 2011). In the absence of clearer indication that the Second Amendment codified a generally recognized right to carry arms in public for self-defense, I would leave this judgment in the hands of the State of Illinois.

Drake v. Filko — 2013

A group of people, referred to as the Appellants, challenged a New Jersey gun regulation requiring permits the carry handguns in public. Again, the District Court said that the laws did not infringe upon anyone's Second Amendment Rights, and again the case made it to the United States Court of Appeals, Third Circuit.

Ruggero J. Aldisert

US Court of Appeals for the Third Circuit 1968-2014

Courtesy Wikimedia Commons

This time Judge Aldisert wrote the decision. They followed the two-step approach set by United States v. Marzzarella based on D.C. v. Heller.

First, we ask whether the challenged law imposes a burden on conduct falling within the scope of the Second Amendment's guarantee.... If it does not, our inquiry is complete. If it does, we evaluate the law under some form of means-end scrutiny. If the law passes muster under that standard, it is constitutional. If it fails, it is invalid.

And again, they determine that the law in question does not contradict the Second Amendment.

Here, we conclude that the requirement that applicants demonstrate a "justifiable need" to publicly carry a handgun for self-defense qualifies as a "presumptively lawful," "longstanding" regulation and therefore does not burden conduct within the scope of the Second Amendment's guarantee. Accordingly, we need not move to the second step of Marzzarella.

For the sake of completeness and the importance of understanding the Second Amendment, they also evaluate the second step.

Nevertheless, because of the important constitutional issues presented, we believe it to be beneficial and appropriate to consider whether the "justifiable need" standard withstands the applicable intermediate level of scrutiny. We conclude that even if the "justifiable need" standard did not qualify as a "presumptively lawful," "longstanding" regulation, at step two of Marzzarella it would withstand intermediate scrutiny, providing a second, independent basis for concluding that the standard is constitutional.

They determined that even after applying the scrutiny of the second step, the law still did not infringe upon Second Amendment rights.

We conclude that the District Court correctly determined that the requirement that applicants demonstrate a "justifiable need" to publicly carry a handgun for self-defense qualifies as a "presumptively lawful," "longstanding" regulation and therefore does not burden conduct within the scope of the Second Amendment's guarantee. We conclude also that the District Court correctly determined that even if the "justifiable need" standard fails to qualify as such a regulation, it nonetheless withstands intermediate scrutiny and is therefore constitutional. Accordingly, we will affirm the judgment of the District Court.

In this case, there was a dissenting opinion provided by Judge Hardiman, who dissented because he felt that the law conditioning the issue of a permit to carry a handgun in public on a showing of a "justifiable need" conflicted with the Second Amendment.

Caetano v. Massachusetts — 2016

In Massachusetts, a woman was arrested for being in possession of a stun gun, which she had for self-defense against an abusive boyfriend. The Massachusetts court said that her ability to own a gun wasn't covered under the Second Amendment because it wasn't a type of weapon that counted as "arms" when the Constitution was written and is not currently accepted as a type of arms required for use in the military. When it reached the Supreme Court, D.C. v. Heller, and McDonald v. Chicago (remember, both 5–4 decisions) were referenced. It was unanimously decided that the type of arms didn't matter, so the Massachusetts Supreme Judicial Court was overruled.

The right of self-defense and the castle doctrine are not dependent upon the Second Amendment; they have a stronger relationship to the Fourth Amendment.

New York State Rifle & Pistol Association v. Bruen — 2022

This case was another challenge to a state gun control act, the Sullivan Act from New York State from 1911 that stood for more than 100 years. The Sullivan Act required a license for possessing firearms small enough to be concealed in public, usually obtained only after a background check and a gun safety class.

Clarence Thomas

US Court of Appeals for the D.C. Circuit
1990-1991

Supreme Court of the United States
1991-

Courtesy Wikimedia Commons

The Supreme Court, in an opinion written by Justice Clarence Thomas, said that the ability to carry a pistol in public was a constitutional right under the Second Amendment. By this point, the court's makeup had changed, so the decision was 6–3 instead of 5–4.

This not only invalidated the 100-year-old law from New York State, but it also gave credibility to these types of laws, often named "Constitutional Carry" laws, despite no previously recognized relationship to the US Constitution.

Justice Thomas's opinion was almost entirely built upon the Heller decision. He says:

In Heller and McDonald, we held that the Second and Fourteenth Amendments protect an individual right to keep and bear arms for self-defense. In doing so, we held unconstitutional two laws that prohibited the possession and use of handguns in the home. In the years since, the Courts of Appeals have coalesced around a "two-step" framework for analyzing Second Amendment challenges that combines history with means-end scrutiny. The Court rejects that two-part approach as having one step too many

Despite the two-step framework originating from the Heller decision, he promptly declines using that approach. Instead, he claims that "*when the Second Amendment's plain text covers an individual's conduct, the Constitution presumptively protects that conduct.*" He continues with:

the government must demonstrate that the regulation is consistent with this Nation's historical tradition of firearm regulation. Only if a firearm regulation is consistent with this Nation's historical tradition may a court conclude that the individual's conduct falls outside the Second Amendment's "unqualified command."

In this, he references Konigsberg v. State Bar of California from 1961, which has the following:

Finally, petitioner argues that, in any event, he was privileged not to respond to questions dealing with Communist Party membership because they unconstitutionally impinged upon rights of free speech and association protected by the Fourteenth Amendment.

At the outset, we reject the view that freedom of speech and association (NAACP v. Alabama, 357 U. S. 449, 357 U. S. 460), as protected by the First and Fourteenth Amendments, are "absolutes," not only in the undoubted sense that, where the constitutional protection exists it must prevail, but also in the sense that the scope of that protection must be gathered solely from a literal reading of the First Amendment. [Footnote 10] Throughout its history, this Court has consistently recognized at least two ways in which constitutionally protected freedom of speech is narrower than an unlimited license to talk. On the one hand, certain forms of speech, or speech in certain contexts, has been considered outside the scope of constitutional protection.

The referenced case was not about the Second Amendment, it was about whether an applicant to the California Bar's denial violated his Fourteenth Amendment rights. The Second Amendment is mentioned in Footnote 10:

That view, which, of course, cannot be reconciled with the law relating to libel, slander, misrepresentation, obscenity, perjury, false advertising, solicitation of crime, complicity by encouragement, conspiracy, and the like, is said to be compelled by the fact that the commands of the First Amendment are stated in unqualified terms: "Congress shall make no law . . . abridging the freedom of speech, or of the press; or the right of the people peaceably to assemble. . . ." But as Mr. Justice Holmes once said:

"[T]he provisions of the Constitution are not mathematical formulas having their essence in their form; they are organic living institutions transplanted from English soil. Their significance is vital, not formal; it is to be gathered not simply by taking the words and a dictionary, but by considering their origin and the line of their growth."

Gompers v. United States, 233 U. S. 604, 233 U. S. 610. In this connection, also compare the equally unqualified command of the Second Amendment: "the right of the people to keep and bear arms shall not be infringed." And see United States v. Miller, 307 U. S. 174.

Thus, the only mention of the Second Amendment in Justice Thomas's reference is a footnote reference to United States v. Miller, and it doesn't get into what the Second Amendment means one way or another. He stresses that the Second Amendment is about "an individual right to keep and bear arms" but doesn't clarify what that means. All interpretations say that the Second Amendment is about an individual right to keep and bear arms, but the historical interpretation is that keeping and bearing arms has to do with forming a militia, and the newer interpretation introduced at the Supreme Court level in D.C. v Heller is that keeping and bearing arms has to do with personal gun ownership. Saying that the Second Amendment is about "an individual right to keep and bear arms" does not advance either argument.

His other point about the "historical tradition of firearm regulation" is also not a strong argument in claiming that firearm regulation is unconstitutional because even though the Federal government didn't have modern gun laws until 1938, States across the Union did have firearm regulation laws. On July 30, 1619 (well before the Second Amendment was ratified in 1791), the General Assembly of Virginia enacted the following into law:

That no man do sell or give any Indians any piece, shot, or powder, or any other arms offensive or defensive, upon pain of being held a traitor to the colony and of being hanged as soon as the fact is proved, without all redemption.

In 1837 Georgia banned selling or "bearing" Bowie knives, pistols, dirks, sword canes, and spears. In 1838 Tennessee banned the sale of Bowie knives and Arkansas toothpicks (a type of heavy dagger). Then in 1879, Tennessee made it illegal to carry pistols other than navy or army pistols, followed by several additional restrictions over the next few years. In 1871 Texas banned handguns in towns. In 1881 Arkansas made it illegal to *"furnish to any person any dirk or bowie knife, or a sword or a spear in a cane, brass or metal knucks, or any pistol of any kind whatever, except such as are used in the army or navy of the United States, ... or any kind of cartridge for any pistol."* In 1876, Wyoming banned bearing firearms or deadly weapons within any city, town, or village limit. In 1901, Kansas said it could prohibit and punish the carrying of firearms or other deadly weapons. This is by no means a comprehensive list; other laws mandated the confiscation of guns for hunting out of season, and several more banned the carrying of firearms within specific areas. There is a long history of gun regulations across the states restricting brandishing weapons, concealed carry, dangerous and unusual weapons, dueling, banning certain individuals from bearing arms, firing weapons, hunting, manufacturing, sales of firearms and/or gunpowder, and more (see [Firearms and Weapons Legislation up to the Early 20th Century](#) in References).When Justice Thomas says that gun regulations should be "consistent with this Nation's historical tradition," there's a plethora of gun regulations to review in US history that establish that tradition that stretches from well before the US Constitution, let alone the Second Amendment, to past the incorporation doctrine established after the 14th Amendment, all the way to today.

Part of the historical inquiry that Justice Thomas proposes is to use reasoning by analogy to determine if a modern gun regulation is "relevantly similar" to a historical one. He gives the following example:

For instance, a green truck and a green hat are relevantly similar if one's metric is "things that are green." See ibid. They are not relevantly similar if the applicable metric is "things you can wear."

He clarifies that this method won't always work.

To be clear, analogical reasoning under the Second Amendment is neither a regulatory straightjacket nor a regulatory blank check. On the one hand, courts should not "uphold every modern law that remotely resembles a historical analogue," because doing so "risk[s] endorsing outliers that our ancestors would never have accepted." Drummond v. Robinson, 9 F. 4th 217, 226 (CA3 2021). On the other hand, analogical reasoning requires only that the government identify a well-established and representative historical analogue, not a historical twin. So even if a modern-day regulation is not a dead ringer for historical precursors, it still may be analogous enough to pass constitutional muster.

Throughout his opinion, he keeps returning to the Heller decision, despite the apparent focus on historical meaning.

Moreover, confining the right to "bear" arms to the home would make little sense given that self-defense is "the central component of the [Second Amendment] right itself." Heller, 554 U. S., at 599; see also McDonald, 561 U. S., at 767. After all, the Second Amendment guarantees an "individual right to possess and carry weapons in case of confrontation," Heller, 554 U. S., at 592, and confrontation can surely take place outside the home.

Although we remarked in Heller that the need for armed self-defense is perhaps "most acute" in the home, id., at 628, we did not suggest that the need was insignificant elsewhere. Many Americans hazard greater danger outside the home than in it. See Moore v. Madigan, 702 F.3d 933, 937 (CA7 2012) ("[A] Chicagoan is a good deal more likely to be attacked on a sidewalk in a rough neighborhood than in his apartment on the 35th floor of the Park Tower"). The text of the Second Amendment reflects that reality.

Justice Thomas was trying to establish (for the first time at a Supreme Court level) that the Second Amendment is about self-defense both within and outside the home. He uses his new interpretation of the Second Amendment being about self-defense when he says:

With these principles in mind, we turn to respondents' historical evidence. Throughout modern Anglo-American history, the right to keep and bear arms in public has traditionally been subject to well-defined restrictions governing the intent for which one could carry arms, the manner of carry, or the exceptional circumstances under which one could not carry arms. But apart from a handful of late-19th-century jurisdictions, the historical record compiled by respondents does not demonstrate a tradition of broadly prohibiting the public carry of commonly used firearms for self-defense. Nor is there any such historical tradition limiting public carry only to those law-abiding citizens who demonstrate a special need for self-

defense.[9]

In note 9, Justice Thomas says that existing gun regulations in 43 states are unconstitutional and that he disagrees with the Drake v. Filko decision of the United States Court of Appeals.

To be clear, nothing in our analysis should be interpreted to suggest the unconstitutionality of the 43 States' "shall-issue" licensing regimes, under which "a general desire for self-defense is sufficient to obtain a [permit]." Drake v. Filko, 724 F.3d 426, 442 (CA3 2013) (Hardiman, J., dissenting). Because these licensing regimes do not require applicants to show an atypical need for armed self-defense, they do not necessarily prevent "law-abiding, responsible citizens" from exercising their Second Amendment right to public carry. District of Columbia v. Heller, 554 U.S. 570, 635 (2008).

This shows the scope of the direction change that the Heller and Bruen decisions take and their potential impact on the country. Justice Thomas doesn't just disagree with the Court of Appeals; he's also trying to invalidate laws in 43 of 50 states with this one decision.

State v. Wilson — 2024

In Hawaii, Christopher Wilson was caught trespassing on private property, the property owner detained Wilson and his two companions with an AR-15 assault rifle until police arrived. When the police arrived, Wilson volunteered that he had a concealed pistol. They found that he did not have a permit to own the handgun, nor had he ever applied for a permit.

Wilson did not follow HRS § 134-9 (The chief of police shall grant licenses to those seeking to carry a pistol or revolver, and the guidelines for when to do so), but was charged for not following HRS § 134-25(a) (properly keeping firearms at your home, work or sojourn; not doing so is a class B felony) and § 134-27(a) (properly keeping ammunition at your home, work or sojourn; not doing so is a misdemeanor).

Wilson argued that three state laws went against the Second Amendment of the US Constitution and Article I Section 17 of the Hawaii Constitution. Article 1 Section 17 of the Hawaii State Constitution is:

A well regulated militia being necessary to the security of a free state, the right of the people to keep and bear arms shall not be infringed.

Justice Todd W. Eddins wrote the court's ruling.

Article I, section 17 of the Hawai'i Constitution mirrors the Second Amendment to the United States Constitution. We read those words differently than the current United States Supreme Court. We hold that in Hawai'i there is no state constitutional right to carry a firearm in public.

...

We reject Wilson's constitutional challenges. Conventional interpretive modalities and Hawai'i's historical tradition of firearm regulation rule out an individual right to keep and bear arms under the Hawai'i Constitution. In Hawai'i, there is no state constitutional right to carry a firearm in public.

Justice Eddins pointed out that the courts had several times, including Young v. Hawaii in 2021, at the Ninth Circuit Court of Appeals, held that the Second Amendment does not provide a right to openly carry a firearm for self-defense.

We hold that the text and purpose of the Hawai'i Constitution, and Hawai'i's historical tradition of firearm regulation, do not support a constitutional right to carry deadly weapons in public.

We conclude that HRS § 134-25 and § 134-27 do not violate Wilson's right to keep and bear arms under article I, section 17 of the Hawai'i Constitution and the Second Amendment to the United States Constitution. Since Wilson lacks standing to challenge HRS § 134-9, we do not take up his Second Amendment challenge to that law.

The Hawaii Supreme Court has a tradition of independence from the Federal Courts, seeing the United States Supreme Court as another source of authority, to be respected, but not binding in cases about interpreting the State Constitution. He quotes State v. Mundon from 2012 where the Hawaii Supreme Court said "*this court has not hesitated to adopt the dissents in U.S. Supreme Court cases when it was believed the dissent was better reasoned than the majority opinion.*" He explains:

State constitutions have a distinct role under our nation's system of federalism. Deciding a case first on state constitutional grounds respects state sovereignty and aligns with a key constitutional design feature – subnational governance.

Thus, they decide to go by the Hawaii State Constitution rather than the United States (even though both are worded identically). Ruling on the interpretation of the State Constitution, he says:

Because the text of article I, section 17, its purpose, and Hawai'i's historical tradition of weapons regulation support a collective, militia meaning, we hold that the Hawai'i Constitution does not afford a right to carry firearms in public places for self-defense.

He then breaks down Article 1 Section 17:

The Second Amendment is nearly identical. Only two commas and three capital letters separate the two.

...

Since article I, section 17 imitates the Second Amendment, it is helpful to look at what the Second Amendment's words mean.

A textual approach to constitutional interpretation appreciates that words appear (or do not) for a reason.

Both clauses of article I, section 17 and the Second Amendment use military-tinged language – "well regulated militia" and "bear arms" - to limit the use of deadly weapons to a military purpose.

In contrast, there are no words that mention a personal right to possess lethal weapons in public places for possible self-defense.

He references Justice Steven's dissenting opinion from D.C. v. Heller, that the first half of the sentence sets the objective of the text and the meaning of the text that follows, and he reasons that the first clause of the state's Article 1 Section 17 does the same, offering context and clarity. He then points out that the phrase "bear arms" from the Founding Era nearly always was used in an unambiguously military sense.

Like the first clause's "well regulated militia," the second clause's "bear arms" has a collective, military meaning. Linguistic experts have churned through historical materials, like the Corpus of Founding Era American English and the Corpus of Early Modern English, to get to the bottom of the Second Amendment's key words.

Justice Eddins also pointed out that the Supreme Court was informed by linguistics researchers for the Bruen decision that the phrase "keep and bear arms" was used in the Founding Era as having a collective, militaristic meaning. He summarizes his review of the text:

No words in article I, section 17 and the Second Amendment describe an individual right. No words mention self-defense.

One of the principles the United States was founded upon was Federalism. Federalism is where power is divided between a central authority over all the territory in a country and separate authorities over territories within that country. Just as Canada is separated into Provinces, the United States is separated into States. While the Federal Government sets laws for the entire country, certain areas of law are often reserved for the governments of those smaller territories. Justice Eddins goes over the importance of federalism principles, and he discusses the conflicts between that and what Justice Thomas said in his Bruen decision:

Bruen snubs federalism principles. Still, the United States Supreme Court does not strip states of all sovereignty to pass traditional police power laws designed to protect people. Wilson has standing to challenge HRS § 134-25(a) and § 134-27(a). But those laws do not violate his federal constitutional rights.

...

Until Heller, the Supreme Court had never ruled that the Second Amendment afforded an individual right to keep and bear arms. Because the Second Amendment provided a collective right, most states conferred an individual right through their constitutions. Federalism principles allow states to provide broader constitutional protection to their people than the federal constitution

Hawai'i chose to use civic-minded language. Article I, section 17 textually cements the right to bear arms to a well regulated militia. Its words confer a right to "keep and bear arms" only in the context of a "well regulated militia."

Article I, section 17 traces the language of the Second Amendment. Those words do not support a right to possess lethal weapons in public for possible self-defense.

He then focuses his attention on the history of Article 1, Section 17, explaining how throughout the state's history it was interpreted as about the militia. For example, the 1968 Constitutional Convention specifically stated:

The Committee feels that reference must be made to the report of the 1950 Constitutional Convention in order that the people of this State not misconstrue the intent of this section. The right to bear arms refers explicitly to the militia and is subject to lawful regulation.

Then in 1978, the Constitutional Convention stated: "[T]he right to keep and bear arms is one enjoyed collectively by members of a state militia"

This was what everyone thought. A 1969 law dictionary explained: the "right to bear arms" refers to the militia, "[n]ot a constitutional right to carry weapons on one's person as a civilian." Right to bear arms, Ballentine's Law Dictionary (3d ed. 1969).

State and federal courts had also, with few exceptions, upheld laws regulating firearms use and possession.

According to Justice Eddins, the Second Amendment's original purpose protects a state's right to have a militia, and until 2008 it always conferred a collective right to bear arms in service to the militia.

There was no individual federal constitutional right to carry deadly weapons in public places for self-defense. There were only statutory, common law, or state constitutional rights.

He points out that the Heller decision wasn't considered sound *"historians quickly debunked Heller's history,"* then reviews Bruen's new standards test of only comparing modern laws to historical laws:

The Supreme Court makes state and federal courts use a fuzzy "history and traditions" test to evaluate laws designed to promote public safety. It scraps the traditional techniques used by federal and state courts to review laws passed by the People to protect people. And by turning the test into history and nothing else, it dismantles workable methods to interpret firearms laws. All to advance a chosen interpretive modality.

...

Bruen's command to find an old-days "analogue" undercuts the other branches' responsibility – at the federal, state, and local levels - to preserve public order and solve today's problems. And it downplays human beings' aptitude for technological advancement.

Time-traveling to 1791 or 1868 to collar how a state regulates lethal weapons – per the Constitution's democratic design - is a dangerous way to look at the federal constitution.

We believe it is a misplaced view to think that today's public safety laws must look like laws passed long ago. Smoothbore, muzzle-loaded, and powder-and-ramrod muskets were not exactly useful to colonial era mass murderers. And life is a bit different now, in a nation with a lot more people, stretching to islands in the Pacific Ocean.

Regulations like storing powder safely, reporting with guns for militia "musters" (weapons inspection), and loyalty oaths are hardly helpful to address contemporary gun violence. Yet those odd laws have historical and traditional roots. Democratically-vetted laws, though – measures taken by today's citizens to save lives - are mostly out of bounds.

...

As the world turns, it makes no sense for contemporary society to pledge allegiance to the founding era's culture, realities, laws, and understanding of the Constitution.

Justice Eddins clearly, and in great detail, explained how the Supreme Court's new interpretations of the Second Amendment since 2008 are inaccurate. His stance is that Judges are not historians, and this relates to Justice Thomas's interpretation that the Second Amendment means that gun laws should only be legal today if similar laws existed when the Second Amendment was ratified. *"Excavating 18th and 19th century experiences to figure out how old times control 21st century life is not a judge's forte."*

Not only that, but he says that the two relevant Hawaii laws do not oppose the Bruen interpretation, as even it says that the right in the Second Amendment is not unlimited and that the right is not a right to keep and carry any weapons whatsoever in any manner whatsoever and for whatever purpose.

After the Supreme Court of Hawaii shared its decision, the petitioners asked the United States Supreme Court to hear the case. While the Supreme Court refused to hear the case (Leaving the Hawaii Supreme Court's ruling in place) some of the Justices did comment on the case.

Justice Thomas, joined by Justice Alito, said that the Hawaii Supreme Court ignored their interpretation of the Second Amendment from Bruen. He called state requirements of gun licenses "licensing regimes" and "schemes." He expressed his frustration with the lower courts not being able to understand the new Second Amendment he invented in the Bruen decision:

The decision below is the latest example of a lower court "fail[ing] to afford the Second Amendment the respect due an enumerated constitutional right."

...

By invoking state standing law to dodge Wilson's constitutional challenge, the Hawaii Supreme Court failed to give the Second Amendment its due regard.

In response to Justice Eddins saying that Wilson's challenge to one of the three laws had no standing because there was nothing to charge with concerning that statute, Justice Thomas says:

> *a state-law holding that a defendant "lacked standing to attack the constitutionality of the ordinance because [he] made no attempt to secure a permit under it" is "not an adequate nonfederal ground of decision" where the "ordinance . . . on its face violates the Constitution."*

> *...*

> *The Hawaii regime's obvious unconstitutionality may be why the Hawaii Legislature has since amended the State's licensing statute to create a "shall issue" regime, at least for concealed carry. The new regime allows any applicant who meets certain baseline requirements to obtain a license without any "special need" limitation.*

To explain a bit about why the United States Supreme Court was not overturning the ruling from the Hawaii Supreme Court, Justice Thomas says:

> *All this said, correction of the Hawaii Supreme Court's error must await another day. Wilson moved to dismiss only some of his charges, most notably leaving for trial a trespassing charge on which his Second Amendment defense has no bearing. He thus seeks review of an interlocutory order over which we may not have jurisdiction.*

He concludes by reiterating his dislike of firearms licensing:

> *In an appropriate case, however, we should make clear that Americans are always free to invoke the Second Amendment as a defense against unconstitutional firearms-licensing schemes. Perhaps Wilson himself will present that case, should he file a post-trial petition for certiorari. Regardless, this issue is an important and recurring one.*

Justice Gorsuch also wrote a statement. He starts by pushing the new logic in the Bruen decision:

> *The Hawaii Supreme Court's decision raises serious questions.*

For one, the court failed to address Mr. Wilson's contention that Hawaii's prosecution is inconsistent "with this Nation's historical tradition of firearm regulation" and so defies the Second Amendment.

Then disagrees with Justice Thomas about state licensing "regimes," saying they only sometimes violate the Second Amendment, rather than all the time.

But it's just as true that state licensing regimes can sometimes be so restrictive that they violate the Second Amendment.

In the end, Justice Gorsuch softens his argument, concluding with the argument not that Wilson's Second Amendment rights were violated, but rather that it wasn't addressed:

In saying that much, I do not mean to suggest Mr. Wilson's Second Amendment defense has merit. I observe only that no one knows the answer to that question because the Hawaii Supreme Court failed to address it.

Despite the complaints by the three United States Supreme Court Justices above, the decision by the Hawaii Supreme Court that the Second Amendment, and Hawaii Constitution Article 1 Section 17, do not imply a right to carry a firearm in public.

Garland, Attorney General, et al. v. Cargill — 2024

The Bureau of Alcohol, Tobacco, Firearms and Explosives (ATF) regulates fully automatic weapons (machine guns) differently than semiautomatic weapons, with fully automatic weapons being more restricted. Fully automatic weapons are typically only used by military personnel. The National Firearms Act of 1934 defines a "machine gun" as "*any weapon which shoots, is designed to shoot, or can be readily restored to shoot, automatically more than one shot, without manual reloading, by a single function of the trigger.*"

After a gunman used semiautomatic rifles equipped with bump stocks to kill 58 people and wound over 500 more in Las Vegas, Nevada, in 2017, the ATF proposed a rule that would "clarify" that semiautomatic weapons equipped with bump stocks qualify as machine guns. A weapon equipped with a bump stock achieves its fully automatic state in a different method than a traditional machine gun, as the mechanism that fires the next shot is not inside the weapon, it depends on the recoil action to cause the trigger to fire again without the welder moving their trigger finger. The user only has to pull the trigger back once, but mechanically the trigger is being pulled multiple times.

Michael Cargill surrendered two of his bump stocks to ATF under protest, then filed suit to challenge the rule. This case was about if a semiautomatic weapon with a bump stock qualifies as a machine gun under the law, and thus can be regulated in the same ways.

Justice Thomas wrote the 6-3 majority opinion which sided with Cargill, that a semiautomatic rifle equipped with a bump stock is not a "machine gun." He provides a variety of reasons, including that the ATF ruled differently in the past, and describing "bump shooting" as a skill that the bump stock merely assists with, but the core reasoning is that the trigger itself is pulled multiple times.

Justice Alito wrote a concurring opinion, in which he says "*There can be little doubt that the Congress that enacted 26 U. S. C. §5845(b) would not have seen any material difference between a machinegun and a semiautomatic rifle equipped with a bump stock. But the statutory text is clear, and we must follow it.*"

Sonia Sotomayor

US District Court for the S.D. of New York 1992-1998

US Court of Appeals for the Second Circuit 1998-2009

Supreme Court of the United States 2009-

Courtesy Wikimedia Commons

Justice Sotomayor wrote the dissenting opinion, which Justice Kagan and Justice Jackson joined. She pointed out that the Trump Administration had widespread bipartisan support when they implemented the bump stock ban, and criticized the majority opinion for being inconsistent with the meaning and purpose of the statutory text. She stated, "*When I see a bird that walks like a duck, swims like a duck, and quacks like a duck, I call that bird a duck. A bump-stock-equipped semiautomatic rifle fires "automatically more than one shot, without manual reloading, by a single function of the trigger." §5845(b). Because I, like Congress, call that a machinegun, I respectfully dissent.*"

She quoted Justice Thomas from McDonald v. Chicago, where he said at the time "*Statements by legislators can assist . . . to the extent they demonstrate the manner in which the public used or understood a particular word or phrase*" and provided several references of Congress contradicting the majority's interpretation. She also pointed out that the Supreme Court had previously read the definition of "machine gun" in the statute to refer to the action of the shooter rather than the firing mechanism, naming Staples v. United States (also written by Justice Thomas). The footnote at the start of the Staples v. United States decision reads:

As used here, the terms "automatic" and "fully automatic" refer to a weapon that fires repeatedly with a single pull of the trigger. That is, once its trigger is depressed, the weapon will automatically continue to fire until its trigger is released or the ammunition is exhausted. Such weapons are "machineguns" within the meaning of the Act. We use the term "semiautomatic" to designate a weapon that fires only one shot with each pull of the trigger, and which requires no manual manipulation by the operator to place another round in the chamber after each round is fired.

Despite news stories surrounding this case trying to relate it to the Second Amendment, nothing in the Court's opinions in Garland, Attorney General, et al. v. Cargill, or Staples v. United States mentions or defines the Second Amendment of the US Constitution. The case instead was over if the ATF had the authority to make the change in classification or if that change should have come from Congress.

United States v. Rahimi — 2024

In this case, the court reviewed a federal statute (18 U. S. C. §922(g)(8)) that infringes upon the right to own a gun if the person in question is subject to a domestic violence restraining order and has threatened the use of physical force on their spouse or their spouse's children.

The defendant, Rahimi, did not argue that the restraining order against him didn't meet the statutory criteria. The restraining order in question had been filed after Rahimi fired shots in his girlfriend's direction in a parking lot. Instead, he argued that the law violates the Second Amendment.

The Federal Statute held up in an 8 to 1 decision, with Clarence Thomas as the only dissenting voice. Unusually, there were seven opinions written by the Justices, six concurring and Thomas's dissent.

John Roberts

US Court of Appeals for the D.C. Circuit
2003-2005

Supreme Court of the United States
2005-

Courtesy Wikimedia Commons

Chief Justice Roberts delivered the majority opinion, in which the Bruen version of the Second Amendment was used...

In Bruen, we explained that when a firearm regulation is challenged under the Second Amendment, the Government must show that the restriction "is consistent with the Nation's historical tradition of firearm regulation." Id., at 24.

...

Since the founding, our Nation's firearm laws have included provisions preventing individuals who threaten physical harm to others from misusing firearms. As applied to the facts of this case, Section 922(g)(8) fits comfortably within this tradition.

He quoted the Heller decision to point out "*that the right was not a right to keep and carry any weapon whatsoever in any manner whatsoever and for whatever purpose*" and this was the primary basis of his argument. The US has a long history of laws meant to protect the public from gun use by those who pose a threat to the physical safety of Americans.

Our analysis starts and stops with Section 922(g)(8)(C)(i) because the Government offers ample evidence that the Second Amendment permits the disarmament of individuals who pose a credible threat to the physical safety of others.

...

From the earliest days of the common law, firearm regulations have included provisions barring people from misusing weapons to harm or menace others.

Justice Roberts defines two different categories of Constitutional gun laws:

1. Surety Laws – **Laws** that require some sort of assurances that the person in question will behave appropriately. Such as being vouched for, or posting a bond. "*While communities sometimes resorted to public shaming or vigilante justice to chastise abusers, sureties provided the public with a more measured solution.*" In order to require a bond for going armed, there would need to be a credible fear that they could cause harm with those firearms.
2. Going-armed Laws – Prohibiting going around armed

with dangerous or unusual weapons that would disrupt the 'public order'. He mentions four states, — Massachusetts, New Hampshire, North Carolina, and Virginia, which had going-armed prohibitions.

Taken together, the surety and going armed laws confirm what common sense suggests: When an individual poses a clear threat of physical violence to another, the threatening individual may be disarmed.

He concludes that the law in question is similar enough to those past laws to hold up to scrutiny.

Like the surety and going armed laws, Section 922(g)(8)(C)(i) applies to individuals found to threaten the physical safety of another.

And also concludes that the statute, and penalty, conform to regulatory tradition.

Interestingly, Chief Justice Roberts says:

In Heller, McDonald, and Bruen, this Court did not "undertake an exhaustive historical analysis . . . of the full scope of the Second Amendment." Bruen, 597 U. S., at 31. Nor do we do so today.

In Justice Sotomayor's concurring opinion, she opens with her continued belief that the Bruen case was wrongly decided, and then explains why the Federal Statute still holds under the Bruen logic.

In short, the Court's interpretation permits a historical inquiry calibrated to reveal something useful and transferable to the present day, while the dissent would make the historical inquiry so exacting as to be useless, a too-sensitive alarm that sounds whenever a regulation did not exist in an essentially identical form at the founding.

...

The Court today clarifies Bruen's historical inquiry and rejects the dissent's exacting historical test. I welcome that development. That being said, I remain troubled by Bruen's myopic focus on history and tradition, which fails to give full consideration to the real and present stakes of the problems facing our society today.

She clarifies that she believes the means-end approach to Second Amendment analysis is the right one (looking at the primary purpose of the Second Amendment rather than looking at historical laws to understand the Second Amendment).

In Justice Gorsuch's concurring opinion, he argues that the Framers understood that the Second Amendment wasn't to be applied blindly, that it was risky and applied within a specific scope: to preserve liberty.

When the people ratified the Second Amendment, they surely understood an arms-bearing citizenry posed some risks. But just as surely they believed that the right protected by the Second Amendment was itself vital to the preservation of life and liberty.

...

through surety laws and restrictions on "going armed," the people in this country have understood from the start that the government may disarm an individual temporarily after a "judicial determinatio[n]" that he "likely would threaten or ha[s] threatened another with a weapon."

...

the challenged law does not diminish any aspect of the right the Second Amendment was originally understood to protect.

Neil McGill Gorsuch

US Court of Appeals for the Tenth Circuit 2006-2017

Supreme Court of the United States 2017-

Courtesy Wikimedia Commons

Justice Gorsuch then takes the time to point out that the two-step approach to Second Amendment cases adopted by the lower courts based on the Heller decision was incorrect. He also further clarifies the point Chief Justice Roberts made about how they were not discussing the full scope of the Second Amendment:

We do not resolve any of those questions (and perhaps others like them) because we cannot. Article III of the Constitution vests in this Court the power to decide only the "'actual cas[e]'" before us, "'not abstractions.'"

Brett Kavanaugh

US Court of Appeals for the D.C. Circuit 2006-2018

Supreme Court of the United States 2018-

Justice Kavanaugh provides historical context in his concurring opinion, starting with:

The Framers of the Constitution and Bill of Rights wisely sought the best of both worlds: democratic self-government and the protection of individual rights against excesses of that form of government. In justiciable cases, this Court determines whether a democratically enacted law or other government action infringes on individual rights guaranteed by the Constitution. When performing that Article III duty, the Court does not implement its own policy judgments about, for example, free speech or gun regulation. Rather, the Court interprets and applies the Constitution by examining text, pre-ratification and post-ratification history, and precedent. The Court's opinion today does just that, and I join it in full.

He reveals that he is an originalist, and goes over what he sees the court's role is in interpreting the Constitution and applying it to the law.

The first and most important rule in constitutional interpretation is to heed the text—that is, the actual words of the Constitution—and to interpret that text according to its ordinary meaning as originally understood.

And points out that all rights discussed in the Constitution are recognized to have exceptions.

Read literally, those Amendments might seem to grant absolute protection, meaning that the government could never regulate speech or guns in any way. But American law has long recognized, as a matter of original understanding and original meaning, that constitutional rights generally come with exceptions.

He makes a point to contradict Justice Sotomayor's interpretation of the Second Amendment:

Some say that courts should determine exceptions to broadly worded individual rights, including the Second Amendment, by looking to policy. Uphold a law if it is a good idea; strike it down if it is not. True, the proponents of a policy-based approach to interpretation of broadly worded or vague constitutional text usually do not say so explicitly (although some do). Rather, they support a balancing approach variously known as means-end scrutiny, heightened scrutiny, tiers of scrutiny, rational basis with bite, or strict or intermediate or intermediate plus or rigorous or skeptical scrutiny.

He says that kind of balancing approach to constitutional interpretation departs from what the Framers wanted, or what the courts should do. The historical comparison method is not perfect, he says, but it can keep judges acting more like umpires than players.

Amy Coney Barrett

US Court of Appeals for the Seventh Circuit 2017-2020

Supreme Court of the United States 2020-

Courtesy Wikimedia Commons

In Justice Barrett's concurring opinion, she starts by agreeing that the right protected by the Second Amendment has limits.

Despite its unqualified text, the Second Amendment is not absolute. It codified a pre-existing right, and preexisting limits on that right are part and parcel of it.

She reviews the concepts of originalism, and how they apply to this case. She also chastises the lower courts for not understanding the Bruen decision, similar to the comments Justice Thomas and Justice Gorsuch have made about how the lower courts did not understand the Heller decision.

She confirms that the court's decision here was the right one:

Here, though, the Court settles on just the right level of generality: "Since the founding, our Nation's firearm laws have included provisions preventing individuals who threaten physical harm to others from misusing firearms."

But then echoes the idea that the full scope and meaning of the Second Amendment is not covered here.

Harder level-of-generality problems can await another day.

Ketanji Brown Jackson

US District Court for the D.C. Circuit
2013-2021

US Court of Appeals for the D.C. Circuit
2021-2022

Supreme Court of the United States
2022-

Courtesy Wikimedia Commons

Justice Jackson's concurring opinion echoes Justice Sotomayor's disagreement with the Bruen decision.

I disagree with the methodology of that decision; I would have joined the dissent had I been a Member of the Court at that time.

...

I write separately because we now have two years' worth of post-Bruen cases under our belts, and the experiences of courts applying its history-and-tradition test should bear on our assessment of the workability of that legal standard. This case highlights the apparent difficulty faced by judges on the ground. Make no mistake: Today's effort to clear up "misunderst[andings]," ante, at 7, is a tacit admission that lower courts are struggling. In my view, the blame may lie with us, not with them.

...

When this Court adopts a new legal standard, as we did in Bruen, we do not do so in a vacuum. The tests we establish bind lower court judges, who then apply those legal standards to the cases before them. In my view, as this Court thinks of, and speaks about, history's relevance to the interpretation of constitutional provisions, we should be mindful that our common-law tradition of promoting clarity and consistency in the application of our precedent also has a lengthy pedigree. So when courts signal they are having trouble with one of our standards, we should pay attention.

...

The message that lower courts are sending now in Second Amendment cases could not be clearer. They say there is little method to Bruen's madness.

She also points out that the Heller decision was disruptive as well, since before Heller the interpretation had been considered settled for over two hundred years, but the Bruen decision puts an excessive burden on the courts to sift through centuries of historical records.

And the unresolved questions hardly end there. Who is protected by the Second Amendment, from a historical perspective? To what conduct does the Second Amendment's plain text apply? To what historical era (or eras) should courts look to divine a historical tradition of gun regulation? How many analogues add up to a tradition? Must there be evidence that those analogues were enforced or subject to judicial scrutiny? How much support can nonstatutory sources lend? I could go on—as others have.

...

I concur in today's decision applying Bruen. But, in my view, the Court should also be mindful of how its legal standards are actually playing out in real life. We must remember that legislatures, seeking to implement meaningful reform for their constituents while simultaneously respecting the Second Amendment, are hobbled without a clear, workable test for assessing the constitutionality of their proposals. See Tr. of Oral Arg. 54–57; cf. Bruen, 597 U. S., at 90–91 (Breyer, J., dissenting). And courts, which are currently at sea when it comes to evaluating firearms legislation, need a solid anchor for grounding their constitutional pronouncements. The public, too, deserves clarity when this Court interprets our Constitution.

In the sole dissenting opinion, Justice Thomas, author of the Bruen opinion, disagrees with the other eight justices that there's a historical comparison to the statute in question.

Not a single historical regulation justifies the statute at issue, 18 U. S. C. §922(g)(8). Therefore, I respectfully dissent.

In opposition to the other Justices who say that the matter isn't currently settled, Justice Thomas says that the Bruen decision settled it.

The Court rejected the means-end-scrutiny approach and laid out the appropriate framework for assessing whether a firearm regulation is constitutional.

He also goes further than what he states in the Bruen decision and says that the right protected by the Second Amendment is absolute.

That Amendment does not merely narrow the Government's regulatory power. It is a barrier, placing the right to keep and bear arms off limits to the Government.

He also contradicts what he said in Bruen, by saying that there is indeed a two-step process:

> Under our precedent, then, we must resolve two questions to determine if §922(g)(8) violates the Second Amendment: (1) Does §922(g)(8) target conduct protected by the Second Amendment's plain text; and (2) does the Government establish that §922(g)(8) is consistent with the Nation's historical tradition of firearm regulation?

According to Justice Thomas, the core purpose of the Second Amendment isn't to maintain liberty, it's to own guns. In contrast to the other Justices in the majority, Justice Thomas says that *"The Government does not offer a single historical regulation that is relevantly similar to §922(g)(8)."* In his opinion, simply because someone is dangerous that's not reason enough to limit their access to guns, and historical laws allowing peaceable citizens to carry guns aren't relevant, neither are safe storage laws where firearms and ammo can be confiscated if it's unsafely stored. He leans on the Heller decision's shift from the Second Amendment being about maintaining liberty through a state militia to being about the personal right to defend yourself, which would thus apply to every individual all the time. While the other Justices have done their best to discuss the nuances of the Second Amendment, Justice Thomas frames it as all or nothing:

> Nearly all firearm regulations can be cast as preventing "irresponsible" or "unfit" persons from accessing firearms. In addition, to argue that a law limiting access to firearms is justified by the fact that the regulated groups should not have access to firearms is a logical merry-go-round.

...

> The Framers and ratifying public understood "that the right to keep and bear arms was essential to the preservation of liberty." McDonald, 561 U. S., at 858 (THOMAS, J., concurring in part and concurring in judgment). Yet, in the interest of ensuring the Government can regulate one subset of society, today's decision puts

at risk the Second Amendment rights of many more. I respectfully dissent.

In their opinions, many of the Justices point out the flaws in Justice Thomas's reasoning. Justice Sotomayor said, "*The dissent reaches a different conclusion by applying the strictest possible interpretation of Bruen.*" Chief Justice Roberts clarified this point:

The dissent reaches a contrary conclusion, primarily on the ground that the historical analogues for Section 922(g)(8) are not sufficiently similar to place that provision in our historical tradition. The dissent does, however, acknowledge that Section 922(g)(8) is within that tradition when it comes to the "why" of the appropriate inquiry. The objection is to the "how." See post, at 18 (opinion of THOMAS, J.). For the reasons we have set forth, however, we conclude that Section 922(g)(8) satisfies that part of the inquiry as well. See supra, at 7, 13–15. As we said in Bruen, a "historical twin" is not required. 597 U. S., at 30.

In summary, the majority, across six different written opinions, stated that the ability to own firearms is limited in scope and that laws restricting the possession of firearms for a limited period if there's a credible threat of that person using those firearms violently are Constitutional and not contrary to the Second Amendment.

Where we are today

Historically the Second Amendment has been interpreted to be about ensuring the existence and the effectiveness of the well-regulated militia, which we know today as the National Guard and Naval Militia. However, we cannot deny that the US Supreme Court changed course and adopted a series of new interpretations starting in 2008 with D.C. v. Heller or that the US Supreme Court could change its opinion yet again in the future. Possibly even to return to the previous interpretation of the Second Amendment they used in every related case before 2008.

Justice Ginsburg was one of many critics of the Heller decision. In an interview with Katie Couric, she said *"Justices continue to think and can change, so I am ever hopeful that if the court has a blind spot today, its eyes will be open tomorrow"*

She also said on a radio interview:

When we no longer need people to keep muskets in their home, then the Second Amendment has no function ... If the Court had properly interpreted the Second Amendment, the Court would have said that amendment was very important when the nation was new; it gave a qualified right to keep and bear arms, but it was for one purpose only – and that was the purpose of having militiamen who were able to fight to preserve the nation.

As the United States Court of Appeals, Third Circuit said, *"[The] Heller [decision] rejected the standards for laws burdening Second Amendment rights."* The courts are still trying to determine how to handle the fluctuating new standards. Heller seemed to set up a two-step process, but then Justice Thomas rejected that idea in the Bruen decision, where he also said that gun regulation laws in 43 states were unconstitutional. On May 17th, 2023, the Supreme Court refused to block a local and state ban on assault weapons in Illinois, so they may be trying to stay out of this debate for a little while to let the lower courts figure out where things settle.

Just as Justice Stevens said of the Roe v. Wade decision being overturned that he believes in the long term, the court will return to recognizing abortions as a necessary procedure that will be performed lawfully, so too perhaps will the Second Amendment return to the original interpretation.

Justice Stevens, in <u>Six Amendments How and Why We Should Change The Constitution</u>, said that for over two hundred years, federal judges uniformly agreed that the Second Amendment only applied to keeping and bearing arms for military purposes and that while it limited the power of the federal government, it did not impose any limits on the powers of states or local government to regulate the ownership or use of firearms. He also made the case that the Heller decision did not prevent Congress from doing better at avoiding multiple killings, such as the one that occurred at Sandy Hook Elementary School in 2012. He said that the Heller decision didn't prevent the regulation of ownership or use of the sorts of automatic weapons often used in those killings and that Heller only protects a subset of weapons for self-defense and only for specific conduct. Concerning the common-law right of self-defense the Supreme Court declared in the Heller decision, he said:

The notion that the states were concerned about possible infringement of that right by the federal government is really quite absurd.

He proposed a new version of the Second Amendment, which slightly changes the meaning, but brings it more in line with what he thought the Framers intended with a lot less ambiguity:

A well regulated Militia, being necessary to the security of a free State, the right of the people to keep and bear Arms when serving in the Militia shall not be infringed.

While that version is certainly less ambiguous, it is also much smaller in the scope of what it protects. With the Stevens version, the National Guard could be made to be under even more control of the Federal Government.

The Second Amendment is there to protect the line between the citizen-soldiers of the state militias and the regulars of the United States standing armies. From the beginning, the distinctions between these two types of military institutions have blurred because of the flexibility of their merging in times of need. We want an independent military to function within the state borders, and for the individual state's interests, and we want those forces available to defend the entire nation. Since the state militias were renamed and reorganized as the National Guard many people can't see the lines of distinction at all, but they are still there and they are still important. We shouldn't abandon the original meanings and intents of the Second Amendment to come up with new meanings because then we may lose the independence the Second Amendment was written to protect. As General John Vessey said in 2001, "*The Regular Army and the National Guard need each other perhaps more than any time in history. The nation needs both in a strong, mutually reinforcing posture.*"

While the National Guard may have evolved through different phases in the last 400 years from local protection and law enforcement to the foundation of the creation of the Continental Army, to what is perhaps the best modern reserve force in the world, it has always played a key role in protecting the freedoms and liberties of all Americans.

There may be nothing wrong with how the Second Amendment is worded now. We, the American People, need to understand and remember what the Second Amendment is for before we go about proposing any changes to it.

US Presidents who served in the Well-Regulated Militia

George Washington

Brigade Commander, Virginia Militia 1753-1758

Commander-in-Chief of Colonial Army 1775-1783

President 1789-1797

Thomas Jefferson

Colonel, Albemarle County Regiment, Virginia Militia 1770-1779

President 1801-1809

James Madison

Colonel, Orange County, Virginia Militia 1775-1776, 1781

Congress of the Confederation 1781-1783, 1786-1787

US House of Representatives 1789–1797

US Secretary of State 1801–1809

President of the United States 1809-1817

James Monroe

Major, Continental Army, 3rd Virginia Regiment 1775-1777

Lieutenant Colonel, Virginia Militia 1777-1780

Colonel of "emergency regiment" of the Virginia Militia 1780

President 1817-1825

Andrew Jackson

Courier, Continental Army 1780

Major General, Tennessee Militia 1801-1821

President 1829-1837

William Henry Harrison

Major General, Kentucky Militia 1812

President for one month of 1841

John Tyler

Captain, Virginia Militia 1813

President 1841-1845

James K. Polk

Captain, Maury County Cavalry, Tennessee Militia, 1812-1825

President 1845-1849

Franklin Pierce

Colonel, New Hampshire Militia
1831-1847

President 1853-1857

James Buchanan

Private, Pennsylvania Militia 1814

President 1857-1861

Abraham Lincoln

Captain, Illinois Militia 1832

President 1861-1865

Ulysses S. Grant

Colonel, Illinois Volunteers 1861-1864

President 1869-1877

Rutherford Hayes

Major General, Ohio Infantry 1861-1865

President 1877-1881

James Garfield

Major General, Ohio Infantry 1861-1865

President seven months of 1881

Chester A. Arthur

Brigadier General, Second Brigade, New York Militia 1857-1863

President 1881-1885

William McKinley

Major, Ohio Volunteers, Union Army 1861-1865

President 1897-1901

Theodore Roosevelt

Captain, Company B, Eighth Regiment, New York National Guard 1882-1886

Colonel, 1st United States Volunteer Cavalry (Rough Riders), United States Army 1898

President 1901-1909

Harry S. Truman

Captain, Missouri National Guard
1905-1906, 1917-1919

President 1945-1953

George W. Bush

First Lieutenant, 147th Fighter Group, Texas Air National Guard 1968-1973

President 2001-2009

(All Presidential Portraits courtesy of the Library of Congress)

References

https://www.nationalguard.mil/about-the-guard/how-we-began/ — National Guard — How we began

https://www.archives.gov/legislative/features/bor — The original proposal for the Bill of Rights, which contained 17 Amendments

https://www.archives.gov/founding-docs/virginia-declaration-of-rights — Virginia Declaration of Rights

https://guides.loc.gov/federalist-papers/text-21-30#s-lg-box-wrapper-25493342 — Federalist 29/Concerning the Militia *Alexander Hamilton*

https://guides.loc.gov/federalist-papers/text-41-50#s-lg-box-wrapper-25493411 — Federalist 46/The Influence of the State and Federal Governments Compared *James Madison*

https://avalon.law.yale.edu/17th_century/england.asp — English Bill of Rights 1689

https://oll.libertyfund.org/page/1789-madison-speech-introducing-proposed-amendments-to-the-constitution — James Madison, Speech Introducing Proposed Constitutional Amendments (1789)

https://www.presidency.ucsb.edu/documents/first-annual-address-congress-0 — First Annual Address to Congress, George Washington

https://harvardlawreview.org/wp-content/uploads/2013/02/vol126_the_people_in_the_constitution.pdf — THE MEANING(S) OF "THE PEOPLE" IN THE CONSTITUTION

https://www.scotusblog.com/wp-content/uploads/2008/01/07-290_amicus_linguists1.pdf — Brief for

Professors of Linguistics and English Dennis E.Barron, Ph.D., Richard W.Bailey, Ph.D. And Jeffery P. Kaplan, Ph.D. In support of petitioners.

https://www.casemine.com/judgement/us/5914cf85add7b04934822172 — Aymette v. State, Tennessee Supreme Court 1840

https://oll.libertyfund.org/title/elliot-the-debates-in-the-several-state-conventions-5-vols — The Debates in the Several State Conventions 5 vols

https://lonang.com/library/reference/story-commentaries-us-constitution/sto-344/ — Commentaries on the Constitution of the United States (1833) *Joesph Story*

https://www.loc.gov/item/98001198/ — The General Principles of Constitutional Law in the United States of America (1880) *Thomas Cooley*

https://tile.loc.gov/storage-services/service/rbc/rbc0001/2012/2012yapam90993/2012yapam90993.pdf — The "Dick" Bill, or Militia Act of 1903.

https://americanenlightenmentproject.org/2nd-amendment-explained/ — 2nd Amendment Explained (abridged vs infringed)

https://www.youtube.com/watch?v=Eya_k4P-iEo&t=1s — Warren Burger interview on PBS News Hour in 1991.

https://www.newspapers.com/clip/102574603/record-searchlight/ — 2nd Amendment has been distorted *article written by Justice Warren E. Burger*

https://harvardlawreview.org/blog/2018/08/corpus-linguistics-and-the-second-amendment/ — Corpus Linguistics and the Second Amendment *Josh Blackman & James C. Phillips*

https://www.monticello.org/research-education/thomas-jefferson-encyclopedia/when-government-fears-people-there-liberty-spurious-quotation/ — The Jefferson Monticello

https://founders.archives.gov/documents/Jefferson/98-01-02-4848 — From Thomas Jefferson to William Short, 8 January 1825

https://www.mountvernon.org/library/digitalhistory/digital-encyclopedia/article/spurious-quotations — Washington Library

https://www.factcheck.org/2019/09/marx-engels-quote-falsely-attributed-to-reagan/ — Factcheck.org, Marx, Engels Quote Falsely Attributed to Reagan

https://supreme.justia.com/cases/federal/us/18/1/ — Houston v. Moore

https://www.archives.gov/milestone-documents/dred-scott-v-sandford — Dred Scott v. Sandford

https://supreme.justia.com/cases/federal/us/60/393/ — Dred Scott v. Sandford

https://www.mtsu.edu/first-amendment/article/58/united-states-v-cruikshank — United States v. Cruikshank (1876)

https://supreme.justia.com/cases/federal/us/92/542/ — United States v. Cruikshank, 92 U.S. 542 (1875)

https://www.pbs.org/newshour/nation/supreme-court-ruling-creates-turmoil-over-gun-laws-in-lower-courts — Supreme Court ruling creates turmoil over gun laws in lower courts

https://www.supremecourt.gov/opinions/21pdf/20-843_7j80.pdf — Bruen decision

https://supreme.justia.com/cases/federal/us/116/252/ — Presser v. Illinois

https://supreme.justia.com/cases/federal/us/552/23/ — Logan v. United States https://supreme.justia.com/cases/federal/us/165/275/ — Robertson v. Baldwin

https://supreme.justia.com/cases/federal/us/279/644/ — United States v. Schwimmer

https://supreme.justia.com/cases/federal/us/293/245/ — Hamilton v. Regents of University of California

https://supreme.justia.com/cases/federal/us/307/174/ — United States v. Miller

https://supreme.justia.com/cases/federal/us/394/812/ — Burton v. Sills

https://supreme.justia.com/cases/federal/us/144/263/ — Logan v. United States, 144 U.S. 263 (1892)

https://supreme.justia.com/cases/federal/us/408/1/ — Laird v. Tatum

https://supreme.justia.com/cases/federal/us/431/494/ — Moore v. City of East Cleveland

https://supreme.justia.com/cases/federal/us/445/55/ — Lewis v. United States

https://casetext.com/case/hickman-v-block?q=81%20F.3d%2098&sort=relevance&p=1&type=case — Hickman v. Block

https://supreme.justia.com/cases/federal/us/521/898/ — Printz v. United States

https://supreme.justia.com/cases/federal/us/524/125/ — Muscarello v. United States

https://law.justia.com/cases/federal/appellate-courts/F3/270/203/545404/ — United States v. Emerson

https://law.justia.com/cases/federal/appellate-courts/F3/312/1052/608831/ — Silveira v. Lockyer

https://supreme.justia.com/cases/federal/us/554/570/ — District of Columbia v. Heller (Supreme Court, 2008)

https://oll.libertyfund.org/page/1619-laws-enacted-by-the-first-general-assembly-of-virginia/ — 1619: Laws enacted by the First General Assembly of Virginia

https://papers.ssrn.com/sol3/papers.cfm?abstract_id=2200991 — Firearms and Weapons Legislation up to the Early 20th Century

https://casetext.com/case/heller-v-district-of-columbia-2 — Heller v. District of Columbia (District Court, 2010)

https://supreme.justia.com/cases/federal/us/561/742/ — McDonald v. City of Chicago

https://casetext.com/case/us-v-marzzarella — U.S. v. Marzzarella

https://supreme.justia.com/cases/federal/us/577/14-10078/ — Caetano v. Massachusetts

https://casetext.com/case/moore-v-madigan-6 — Moore v. Madigan

https://casetext.com/case/drake-v-filko — Drake v. Filko

https://supreme.justia.com/cases/federal/us/597/20-843/ — New York State Rifle & Pistol Association, Inc. v. Bruen

https://www.youtube.com/watch?v=JQRXKP8Iuj0— Interview of Justice Stevens on PBS News Hour in 2019

https://www.supremecourt.gov/opinions/23pdf/22-976new_i4dk.pdf — Garland, Attorney General, et al. v. Cargill

https://www.supremecourt.gov/opinions/23pdf/22-915_806b.pdf — United States v Rahimi

https://casetext.com/case/state-v-wilson-11222528 — State v.

Wilson

https://www.marieclaire.com/politics/news/a10305/ruth-bader-ginsburg-blind-spot/ — Marie Claire, Ruth Bader Ginsburg Says Male Justices Have a Blind Spot On Women's Rights

https://www.loc.gov/free-to-use/presidential-portraits/ — Presidential Portraits, Library of Congress

Further reading

https://giffords.org/lawcenter/gun-laws/second-amendment/the-supreme-court-the-second-amendment — The Supreme Court & the Second Amendment

https://www.washingtonpost.com/archive/opinions/1990/11/04/phantom-second-amendment-rights/f4381818-fed9-4e63-8d62-f62056818181/ — PHANTOM SECOND AMENDMENT 'RIGHTS'

https://www.theatlantic.com/ideas/archive/2020/02/big-data-second-amendment/607186/ — The Mysterious Meaning of the Second Amendment

https://www.cnn.com/2016/08/10/politics/what-does-the-second-amendment-actually-mean-trnd/index.html — 27 words: Deconstructing the Second Amendment

https://www.theatlantic.com/national/archive/2011/06/constitutional-myth-6-the-second-amendment-allows-citizens-to-threaten-government/241298/ — Constitutional Myth #6: The Second Amendment Allows Citizens to Threaten Government

https://illinoislawreview.org/online/the-invention-of-the-right-to-peaceable-carry-in-modern-second-amendment-scholarship/ — The Invention of the Right to 'Peaceable Carry' in Modern Second Amendment Scholarship

https://www.scribd.com/document/695864982/The-Language-and-Grammar-of-the-Second-Amendment — The Language and Grammar of the Second Amendment

https://www.yalelawjournal.org/article/originalism-by-analogy-and-second-amendment-adjudication — Originalism-by-Analogy and Second Amendment

Adjudication
Michael D. Doubler, I am the Guard, 2001

Selected Image Citations

(Cover - Top) Reenactment of Militia and Troops of the American Army at the Battle of Cowpens. Public Domain Image. https://www.goodfreephotos.com/historical-battles/american-revolution/reeneactment-of-militia-and-troops-of-the-american-army-at-the-battle+of-cowpens.jpg.php

(Cover - Bottom) WASHINGTON — National Guard members in process upon arriving in Washington, D.C., on Jan. 7, 2021. National Guard Soldiers and Airmen from Maryland, Virginia, Delaware, Pennsylvania, New York and New Jersey are traveling to the National Capital Region to join the District of Columbia National Guard in supporting federal and district authorities through the inauguration of President-elect Joseph Biden. Photo By: Senior Airman Amanda Bodony. https://www.nationalguard.mil/Resources/Image-Gallery/News-Images/igphoto/2002561562/

Portrait of Thomas Cooley — Photo by Doug Elbinger, Lansing – June 1996, Portrait Artist Ives, L.T. 1885, Michigan Supreme Court Historical Society. https://www.micourthistory.org/special-sessions/presentation-of-the-portrait-of-the-honorable-thomas-m-cooley/

Portrait of Tench Coxe — The Miriam and Ira D. Wallach Division of Art, Prints and Photographs: Print Collection, The New York Public Library. "Tench Coxe" The New York Public Library Digital Collections. 1783 - 1888. https://digitalcollections.nypl.org/items/510d47da-2a83-a3d9-e040-e00a18064a99

(All other Portraits courtesy of the Library of Congress, unless otherwise noted)

(Photos of the National Guard Memorial Museum in Washington D.C. taken in 2024 by Harley Robertson)

www.ingramcontent.com/pod-product-compliance
Lightning Source LLC
Chambersburg PA
CBHW071021240526
45469CB00006BD/2029